BLINDSIGHTED

TURLEY RICHARDS

BLINDSIGHTED
By Turley Richards
ISBN: 978-1-62452-039-6
Insight Publishing
Cover Design: Steve Wilson
Formatting and Layout: Chris Ott

ACKNOWLEDGMENTS

My never-ending thanks to my mother-mom. I hope to see you someday in heaven.

This book would never have come to pass without the help of Laura Leigh Hess and her editing abilities and her endless energy for the editing process before it went to the publisher. Also, the contributions by Richard Desantis—getting everything ready from my transcripts plus one hour a week for almost three years. My thanks to Michele Madgar for transcribing all of my words from a digital recording and actually coining the title. Thanks to David Knuckolls for taking the transcripts and putting them in a folder for easy access for my writings.

There are so many people through my long journey of life that I can't begin to thank them separately. So, to all of you who have touched my life, THANKS.

My mother and my two children and grandchildren will always be my heartbeat, and my heart and soul are filled to the brim with my love for them.

Thanks to Joe Boyland for being a great friend, and for his great knowledge of the music business.

Thanks to Gene Eichelberger, Hall of Fame recording engineer, for teaching me so much to perfect my abilities in the studio.

Thanks to Paul Tannen for sticking with me through three record labels.

Thanks to Lew Merenstein for his incredible production of *I Heard the Voice of Jesus.*

Thanks to my close friends: Jim Bruer, Mickey Clark, Jake Butts, Bob Tiell, Paul Steinmetz, Gene Eichelberger, Joe Boyland, David Knuckolls, the supreme animal lover, Leslie DeBord, and Bill Myers for always being there for me.

Thanks to Kiongazi for needing me, when I truly needed him. Buddy, you were a great dog and wonderful friend. I'll see you and Amari, Barkley, and Kiambi at the rainbow bridge and I'll introduce you to Asia, a beautiful kitten I spent a few months with.

TABLE OF CONTENTS

FOREWORD

My mother's phrase, "defeat is no option," is used often throughout this book. Without my mother's incredible wisdom, and her drive to help me understand that statement as well as live it, I don't think I would have been able to meet all of the challenges life has thrown at me.

Insane and *crazy* are two words that certainly describe my long life's journey, but I can also use *satisfaction* and *fulfillment*. All four of those words also describe show business (or at the very least, the music business). Why would anyone want to go through the recording gauntlet? Our hearts are broken on a continual basis but I guess that's what makes us work that much harder in order to reach the goal we call success.

Any success I achieved was because of my mother. My measure of success is the fact that I made it through all of the total bullshit of this business, and I'm satisfied with my accomplishments. However, my greatest success is that I've always been there for my children. Nothing could pull me away from the love they deserved from their father.

This book covers a lot of memories from 1946, when I lost my left eye to a bow and arrow accident, all the way to 2014. I will admit that I'm sure I messed up some of the dates and small details of the stories throughout all these years. In addition, I suspect I forgot some names, but there are also some names that I changed for a good reason. However, I believe that with the exception of 1968 through 1971 I will be pretty much right on. Those three years have presented a challenge for me to remember everything. They are the last three years of my sight, and I blocked out a lot of it. Writing this book has unlocked some of those doors but some just won't let me in to see it all, and maybe that's a good thing.

I hope that some of you will be inspired by how my mother taught me to never give up, and you might be able to do it as well.

Remember: DEFEAT IS NO OPTION.

"Are you ready, Turley?"

An empty psychologist's office, save for the doctor and his client. They sit opposite each other, the doctor speaking in a low, measured tone. His client arrives nervous but sits back in his chair, his own voice gradually becoming calm and composed. The outer office is quiet. This is the second time the client has undergone hypnosis.

"Yeah, Ven, I'm ready."

"Clear your mind. You are sitting here, and that's all that matters. Even this room will disappear. Take a deep, cleansing breath and focus on my voice. There's nothing to worry about; not even your singing is a concern. Your voice will heal and return. Now, in a few moments, you will tell me what you see . . ."

Ven's voice gradually fades, and Turley is no longer in the room. He describes what he sees: a small boy in pants and a yellow striped shirt, playing with some older kids. The sun is warm on his face, the grass scratching his ankles. There's yelling and laughter. The oldest and biggest boy is holding in his hands a bow and arrow set.

He sees the kids take turns letting the older boy shoot arrows into a pillow they are holding against their backsides. It's now his turn. He watches the little boy hold the pillow against himself as he bends over. Seconds pass, and the boy turns his head and looks back in innocence. He sees the arrow fly across the yard, and strike the little boy in his left eye. The little boy runs toward his house, with his hand over his left eye, the arrow sticking out between his fingers. He sees his Aunt on her porch drop a glass of milk and a sandwich and come toward him. The arrow falls out and blood shoots out of his eye. His yellow shirt is stained, and the stain spreads. His Aunt's knees buckle and she falls to the ground. From the corner of his eye, he sees his mother in the kitchen window, screaming. Her eyes are white with shock and fear. He begins to cry.

The image of the boy is gone.

Turley shakes his head. He sits back and wipes the tears from his eyes, breathing hard.

"I've got to go," he says, "I've got to go see my mom."

"You seem very upset right now. Why don't you sit here and talk with me?"

"I can't. I've got to go see my mom. Oh my God, what that poor woman has gone through. She's always thought it was her fault. That's why I've got to go talk to her."

"Okay, Turley, but will you promise me you will call me tomorrow?"

"Sure, Ven. I'll talk to you then."

CHAPTER 1

*"So, you do what must be done, you keep on holdin' on
to your hopes, your plans, and your dreams.
Hold on, hold on, hold on, to the American dream."*[1]

I was born in South Charleston in 1941. Despite being close to heavy industry, South Charleston held on to a quaint, "Mayberry" charm. Most of the streets in South Charleston were named after numbers or letters, and laid out in a grid. The main roads were also connected by alleys, creating neighborhoods within neighborhoods. The main street was D Street, which began on the railroad and ended at the Indian Mound, a two-story-tall, pre-historic burial chamber credited to the Criel Indians.

In and around D Street were the business and cultural centers of town: the Town Hall, Gorbey's Music, Copper's Drugstore, the high school, the Black Eagle Canteen, and the La Belle Theater.

On one side of the Indian Mound were a basketball court and a concrete stage for summer concerts. Oakes Field served the sports needs of the local schools—a two-thousand-seat stadium of green turf and stone walls. South Charleston was also home to Rock Lake Pool, a unique attraction, built out of an old rock quarry and billed as "the largest and most beautiful pool in the Southeast."

South Charleston also had its own slang, defining locals from the transient. "Going over street" meant going across town from the Black Eagle to the Indian Mound. Going to Charleston was going "uptown."

I was born in a house on E Street, down by the river. Eventually we moved to F Street, up by the railroad. Across the tracks were the heights, "up on the hill" where the wealthier families lived. The heights overlooked town, which my mom said made it easier for the rich folks up there to look down on us.

My parents worked hard to give their five children a good upbringing. My sister Janice was the oldest, followed by Fred, Carolyn, Frank, and me. Our personalities and temperaments were as different from each other as our ages. Like most siblings, we also tended to take after one parent or the other. Janice and I, the oldest and the youngest, were more like Mother while Fred, Carolyn, and Frank, leaned toward Dad.

My father was born Francis Marion Turley into a large family of seven brothers and sisters. The Cody Turley I knew growing up was a hard, gruff, impatient man. He was hard to love and never said, "I love you." In my father's time, men didn't show emotion as easily as they do today. Being a good father and man meant being a good provider. The roof over our heads, the clothes on our backs, and the food on the table was how he expressed his love for

---

[1] *American Dream*, Turley Richards, Kiongazi Music, BMI, 1981.

us. To his credit, he did this well and without complaint. He could also be the best of neighbors, always ready to lend someone in need a helping hand.

My mother was born Sylba Lena Eskew. Two years younger than my father, she was as outgoing, loving, and was as happy-go-lucky as my father was distant. Also unlike my father, my mother was consistent, sharing her good nature equally both in and out of the house. She liked to read and quote the Bible, but her God was of the encouraging, tolerant, and compassionate kind. His Son was sent to teach and save, not judge. The "Word" was a code to live by.

I was the closest to my mom's two younger siblings, Virginia, nicknamed Flossie, who lived next door to us on E Street, and Hubert who lived in St. Albans, a nearby town. I've never been sure where I got my musical talent from but Uncle Hubert, with his guitar and his love of the popular music of the time, would be my best guess. Uncle Hubert was probably the best male role model I had growing up. A tough but gentle "bear," Hubert was just as kind and religious as my mother. He was a war veteran and a decorated war hero who, like many men his age, never talked about what he had witnessed.

My parents' relationship is still a mystery to me. No two people could have been more different. Were they happy together? I have no idea, but in those days people did not divorce each other. My mother liked to make people smile, and it might have been my father's country charm that first attracted her. With only a sixth grade education, she was an unlikely wiz at crossword puzzles. Undereducated herself, mom was proud that my brothers and sisters all went on to college and earned degrees. She also took pride in her work. As a seamstress, she made all of the majorette and cheerleader uniforms for the area schools. Her workshop was our basement on F Street where she would design, cut patterns, and sew an assembly line of fabric and braid. She also made costumes for the local dance schools, her pride of work being rewarded when some of the dancers, and her costumes, made it onto the Ed Sullivan Show.

My mother disciplined in extreme cases with a yardstick, but more often than not her method was a measured, firm voice. That was usually enough to get her point across.

"Now Richard," she would say, "you cut that foolishness out!"

When her firm voice didn't work, she had to resort to creative methods. My brother Frank and I were ten and nine years old when we disappeared one afternoon during a major storm, and were found twelve hours later, and miles away, in the garage of a friend. Dad wanted to whip us, but Mother put her foot down and told him this time she was doling out the punishment.

The next morning, Mother dressed Frank in one of our sister's red velvet dresses with his clodhoppers. I got to wear a blue and pink sun suit with tennis shoes. Mother plopped us on the front porch on a Sunday afternoon, where we had to endure hours of teasing and catcalls from the passersby. Mother's punishment made a much more lasting impression. Frank even said he wished Dad had whipped us instead. We made sure our parents knew where we were for a long time after that.

My mother was that unique person we have all known—a teacher, coach, and mentor, who naturally garnered people's respect. She drew people to her with an innate feeling of love. We listened to her because we wanted to. All of our friends called her "Mom Turley."

My father had a certain country charm, and people he encountered around town knew him as a funny, likeable man. One of his early passions was baseball, and he had used his catcher's build playing for one of the local industrial teams in the semi-pro Twilight League. He seemed fearless, which worked to his advantage when he felt mistreated or wronged.

When he was at home though, he was unpredictable, and we would walk on pins and needles. There was no warning to what might set off his temper, and his fuse was short. He was a physically powerful man, not tall but strong, with long muscular arms and a bull neck. In disciplining us, he was a hitter, and we ran if we knew he was looking for us. There was never any evidence of his abuse toward my mother, and when my brothers and I were older; my father knew that we wouldn't have stood for it. He did work hard to support his family. Cody worked as a skilled pipe fitter for FMC. He was a hard worker, putting in fourteen-hour days between his shift at FMC and his plumbing jobs that eventually became necessary to pay for my medical bills.

My dad was also unusual in that he almost never talked about politics. As a staunch Republican in a Republican state, our joke was that he would have voted for Satan if the fallen angel himself was running for the GOP. With a steely loyalty like his, what was there to talk about? My dad was shaken, however, by Nixon and Watergate, which didn't say much for Nixon. My father became a staunch Democrat the rest of his life.

My dad was a tough guy with a reputation for being unbeatable in a fight. Some of his stories from his younger days made for good entertainment to his male children. One of our favorites was about my dad when he was about twenty-four years old.

Janice was born, and Fred was on the way, so my dad went out with some buddies one night to visit the county fair. He and his friends walked around seeing all of the sideshows and carnival games. In doing so, they ran across a travelling boxer who was taking on any local willing to get in the ring with him. The story went that any local who could last three rounds would get five dollars a round as a prize, but if you defeated him, the pot was $500.

My dad and his friends watched the spectacle for a while, as people they knew entered the ring only to be knocked out in the first round. My dad noticed that every time a guy entered the ring, the big boxer would approach them head on with arms raised in the classic boxer's stance. As the contestant started to circle around him, he went right for the knockout and took them out before they knew what had hit them. Dad decided he had seen enough and entered the ring for his turn. The bell rang, and the boxer began his march toward Dad. Dad flew at the boxer at full speed, and as the boxer's eyes widened in surprise, his jaw also dropped. That's where Dad got him. He hit him square on the jaw while his jaw was open and knocked him out cold. The manager, not realizing that my dad was pretty smart, tried to entice him to go double or nothing. Dad just looked at him and smiled, and said "Hell no! I can't surprise him twice." Dad went home with $500, a small fortune in those days. We were told that money helped the family for almost three years. Of course, he also had to admit where the money came from.

I wonder if Mom used her famous line and said, "Now Cody, you cut that foolishness out!"

"Cody Turley and Silba Turley around 1929."

CHAPTER 2

March 18, 1946

The boy with the bow and arrow was a twelve-year-old neighbor. I was only four and a half, but thrilled to be playing with the bigger kids. Kids don't think they can get hurt. Everyone was laughing and wanted another turn holding up the target. It was fun watching the other kids go ahead of me. Now it was finally my turn, and I bent over and held the pillow to my butt. It seemed to me like it was taking too long. I said "Hey! What's going on?" as I was turning my head to look back. He had released the arrow right as I started to turn my head. The arrow hit and pierced my left eye.

My mom didn't drive, so a neighbor rushed me to South Charleston's Thomas Memorial Hospital, with my mom holding my head back wrapped in a towel. When I arrived, the hospital immediately called a Dr. David Chandler, a respected eye surgeon in Charleston. His line was busy—his secretary taking what turned out to be a personal call. It was 1946 and there were no multi-lined phones, and no call waiting. The hospital staff tried another doctor and my fate, as the saying goes, was sealed.

The doctor they reached was not as skilled as Dr. Chandler neither, as it turned out, did he possess the good physician's most important trait, common sense. But this was unknown to desperate parents whose child was in need of help. In the days that followed the doctor decided, without consulting another specialist, to try to save my hopelessly damaged left eye. If he had consulted a peer, he would have been told that my left eye needed to be removed within forty-eight hours to prevent sympathetic reaction of the right eye, in an effort to overcompensate for the left. Instead he left the eye in for eleven months, which caused the eye to rot and produced a massive infection throughout my body, along with a great loss of vision in my right eye.

My parents, particularly my mother, were still shaken, which might explain their own clouded judgment in trusting this doctor until it was almost too late. The doctor eventually removed my eye, but not until the damage was done and it was too late.

As my condition grew worse, my parents finally lost faith, and on the recommendation of my dad's sister, took me to see Dr. Lyle in Cincinnati, the number one eye doctor in the country at the time. When Dr. Lyle sat in front of me to examine me, he told my mom that my right eye had so much infection behind it, that if he pushed on my face underneath the eye, the entire eye would come out. Dr. Lyle immediately had me admitted to Cincinnati's St. Joseph's Hospital. I was only five years old. The doctor at the hospital told my parents that if something wasn't done immediately to stop the infection, I would die within three weeks. A radical treatment of antibiotics was required. I received fourteen shots a day for twenty-one consecutive days. I made it through the hospital stay, but the doctors told my parents that I would probably have a weakened immune system for the rest of my life, and that the whole procedure would likely stunt my growth. Today, at six foot four and more than two hundred pounds, I guess the joke's on them.

For six years thereafter, I would wake up the whole house with my screaming while I slept. I remember having nightmares where I could hear footsteps coming down the hall. An enormous nurse who took up the entire hallway would be coming toward me holding a huge jousting lance that had a needle sticking out of the end. She would run faster as she came toward me with the needle, and I would start to scream.

I learned years afterward that my father blamed my mother for the accident. "You weren't watching him right," was his accusation. Whenever there were problems caused by my vision, or I needed to prepare for a new surgery, he would remind her saying, "If you had been watching him like you should have been—"

According to him, I was hurt because she wasn't doing her job right as housewife and mother. My mother was already devastated, and she now took this burden solely upon her shoulders. I also learned that my father's infamous temper almost got the best of him when he tried to "go after" the first doctor once he knew how negligently he had treated me. Luckily for the doctor (and probably for my dad), he was out of town at the time, and in the end no action was ever taken against him.

Initially, the parents of the boy who shot the arrow didn't want to admit their son was responsible. They suggested that I must have fallen into a rosebush and punctured my eye. I was later told the arrow slipped from the boy's hand, and he had to reload it. In small town America in 1946, what would have brought criminal charges and a lawsuit today, was dealt with by who would shun whom. After a time, the family felt so ostracized by the neighbors that they moved away.

Since the accident, my mother had been isolated in her grief. I was alive, but what kind of life would I eventually lead? Her baby had nearly died, might go blind, and she shouldered the blame that her husband had laid on her. Whom could she turn to? Aunt Flossie and Uncle Hubert did their best to offer comfort and support, but they couldn't truly understand and she couldn't burden her other children with her anguish. How do you continue to live believing that you are responsible for your child's disability and pain?

On the morning I was to receive my "new eye," my mother had made a decision. Instead of going to the doctor, she planned to go to the Kanawha River and end both of our lives. A future blighted by guilt and heartache would never happen. Irrational and ultimately selfish, suicide also destroys those left behind. By ending our lives, my mother had become blind herself, not seeing—or choosing not to see—that she would be destroying the lives of those she left behind. Faith had deserted her.

My mother got us ready as if to keep my doctor appointment. She dressed me, we left on time, and we even stopped for breakfast. I was nearly six, and after all I had gone through—the hospitals, pain, and fear—I was excited to go out to eat. It was like a holiday and I couldn't be still in my seat, fidgeting and singing until a curious old man in the next booth asked me why I was so happy.

"Why do you have that big bandage?" the old man asked.

"I'm going to the doctor's today with my mother," I answered.

"Well, if I was going to the doctor, I wouldn't be acting so happy."

"Yes you would, if you were me."

"Why?" asked the old man.

"Because today I'm getting a new eye!"

My mother, watching my innocence and hearing my joy, was shaken from her despair. The chance question of an old man and a child's innocent response had saved two lives.

8

She renewed herself and her sacred commitment as a mother. Her faith returned and my challenges were hers. Whatever could be done would be done to save my vision, and defeat was no option.

Throughout my childhood, mother would take me by the shoulders and say to me "Richard, you listen to me! You are not handicapped, and don't you ever let anyone treat you as though you are handicapped!"

I was fated for a different path, and she would encourage and guide me toward happiness. My mother was my angel watching over me. I was blessed. I was safe.

CHAPTER 3

My family's life had been upended. My mother and father would work all they could to cover my medical bills, and my mother would sustain me emotionally with her endless encouragement, wisdom, and love. I was only six so until I got older I would need constant attention, which my mother lavished on me, and I soaked it up. What normal five- or six-year-old wouldn't? Unfortunately, this created resentment from my two closest siblings, Carolyn and Frank. This was understandable since jealousy over a parent's attention can be common, even under normal circumstances. Usually these problems get worked out among siblings as they get older, but we weren't so lucky. My brother and sister never seemed to understand.

My mother insisted that my eyesight was never to be considered a handicap and I would live as normal a life as possible, but I was a handful.

My mom would be asked, "Do you think Richard is too hyper?"

She would answer, "I don't know, why don't you pull him down off the wall and ask him?"

My eldest sister Janice never felt any jealousy or resentment toward me. Janice was already a teenager, but as the eldest, she was asked to look after me sometimes.

"Mother," Janice would laugh, "we were at the La Belle and the movie was playing. I got up for a Coke and when I came back, I couldn't find Richard. Everyone was laughing and pointing toward the stage. Then I saw him up there singing and dancing in front of the movie. Someone yelled, 'Looks like he's gonna be in show business!'"

"Mom! Richard walked away from me in Kroger's and I only found him because there was a crowd of adults around him. He was singing and doing impersonations and I never saw anything so funny in my life!"

Later, after Janice moved away, it was Carolyn who bent Mom's ear:

"Mother, there was a singer on the stage at the Indian Mound and all of my friends were there. Then everyone was pointing at the stage because Richard had taken the microphone. He was singing and dancing with his shirt open and I was never so embarrassed in my life!"

Learning to cope with my needs, we eventually settled into a normal home life. We moved to the corner of First Avenue and F Street where I shared a basement room with my brother Frank. Our room also doubled as my mom's laundry area and sewing room. Our house was next door to an attached row of houses that shared a common back yard. Dad continued to work long hours at FMC and moonlight as a plumber.

He liked to relax by reading the newspaper and following the Cincinnati Reds (back then they were still the Redlegs) and the West Virginia University Basketball team. We had a television with a filament screen meant to give the illusion of color as we watched *Howdy Doody, I Love Lucy,* and *The Adventures of Superman.* Summers were spent swimming at Rock Lake or on Coal River. I played basketball and baseball, and went to movies at the La Belle. Family visits meant seeing my Aunt Flossie, my cousins, my grandparents, and Uncle Hubert, listening to him play his guitar. There was also another eye surgery every year or so. My mother sustained her strength and hope for my sake. She needed strength against the obstacles she knew I would have to face and the day when I might go blind. She hoped that the day, would never come.

Normal vision is 20/20, legally blind is 20/200. My vision was 20/400. Because of the scar tissue in my right eye, glasses never quite worked for me. When I was eventually prescribed contact lenses at twenty-one, my sight improved to 20/70. In the meantime, I learned to cope and compensate.

I had been musical since I was little. My first instrument was a saxophone kazoo. Because of all the surgeries, I was delayed starting school. A bunch of guys at my dad's plant put their money together and gave me a record player, along with twenty 78 rpm records, most of which were big band.

Not long after that, Mother and I were at Field's Five and Dime. It was 1947, and it was the first year that kazoos were shaped like instruments. Field's had a big box of them; my mom told me to reach in and find one that I liked. I found a kazoo that felt different than the others, and held it up for my mom.

"Honey," she said, "that's called a saxophone."

We bought the kazoo. I don't remember a lot about this, but Mother told me that every day while the other kids were at school, I would spend two to three hours listening to those records and playing the kazoo. Looking back, I realize this is where I learned to develop my incredible range, my timing, my pitch, and my ability to scat sing. I was trying to match the different instruments that were playing on the records. This is when I learned the fundamentals that in later years would serve as my formal training.

When I was eleven I acquired my first guitar—a Gene Autry—that I found in the trash. It only had one string, but that didn't stop me from playing it and singing, "Give Me That Old Time Religion," while walking the neighborhood. When others heard me sing for the first time at eleven or twelve years old, they were shocked at the purity and range of my voice. The voice was great, but that guitar was annoying, so the neighbors pooled their money in order to end their own misery. A visit to Gorbey's Music shop for new strings solved that problem. Eventually I graduated to a new electric Fender Stratocaster and amplifier bought from Mr. Herbert's Music in Charleston.

I loved sports, particularly basketball and baseball, and as most boys my age, I dreamed of being Mickey Mantle or Bill Russell. People were concerned if I might get hurt and would ask my mom if it was wise to let me play sports with the other kids. Her response was always, "I'll just wipe his nose for him and send him back. He needs to be prepared for life."

I was going to be an overachiever. I would play basketball twice as hard as the other kids, and I would work harder in school (or at least harder at getting girls to do my work). I would also play hard with my friends, sometimes to the point of recklessness.

"Hey Richard, what the hell are you doing?!"

"C'mon!" I'd yell to everyone, "Let's hitch a ride on that train."

"But it's moving!"

"So what?!"

We'd run alongside the train, slipping on the loose gravel and reaching for the steel ladder as if we were playing on a slide. We chose the slow ones as they pulled out of the freight yards. I'd lead the way up the sheer sides to an open well where coal should be. Better yet, across the top of a boxcar, and then jump from car to car. At ten years old, I doubt if this is what my mom had in mind for me getting "prepared for life."

What happened to me the following year also wasn't part of mother's plan. It wouldn't be part of any parents' plan for their child, and robbed me of the rest of my childhood.

I was eleven and a half, and was spending the night at a friend's house. The friend's mother was single and worked nights, so we were left with a babysitter, who was a nineteen-year-old girl. My friend and I were in the bathtub together playing with toy boats and splashing around when my friend asked me if I had ever played with myself. I hadn't, but my friend had, and he started to demonstrate how to do it. Then he told me it was my turn. I started to do what he had shown me, and the babysitter walked in. She looked angry, and ordered my friend to put on his pajamas and go to his room. She told me to put on my pajamas and go to the living room. I thought we were in deep trouble and I was scared.

She came into the room, and said "What were you doing in there?

"I . . . um . . . he was showing me how to . . . um—"

"What were you doing?"

"Um . . . he called it playing with myself."

She pulled my pajama bottoms down and grabbed me. "I know what you were doing! This is what you were doing," she said as she mimicked the action I had been shown.

"You know, you could go to the Davis Child Shelter for what you were doing in there! Do you want me to tell your mom and dad?"

"No!"

The Davis Child Shelter was a reform school in Charleston that many parents used as a threat in order to make sure their children behaved. They didn't mean it, but we didn't know that, and just the mention of the name was enough to scare most kids around town.

She slid to her knees and took me in her mouth. All I could think was, "Oh my God, that's where I pee from!"

Then she pushed me down on the couch, and I saw that she was naked under her robe. She pulled my face down between her legs and said "lick me."

I was beyond scared and confused. All I could think was that she had put her mouth where I peed, and now she wanted me to do the same thing to her. I told her I wanted to stop, but she again threatened me with the reform school. She rolled me over onto my back, climbed on top of me, and mounted me.

When it was over, she again threatened me that if I told anyone I would be sent to the Davis Child Shelter.

I was too young to possibly understand that I had been raped. Somehow she made me feel ashamed—as though what we had just done was my fault. She also wanted more, and told me when to come over to her house. She said if I didn't do it, she would tell my parents what I had done. I believed her, and I was scared to death. I was a young man in puberty, though, and my fear soon disappeared. So from the age of nearly twelve to fourteen, I began to look forward to leaving school and running to her house when told to. The fun ended when she, of all things, got married. I can't imagine what would have happened if my parents had found out. Although I lived in a state of semi-fear for those years, luckily I still had my music and sports to provide a sense of normalcy and balance things out.

All of the Turley kids were good athletes, particularly in basketball. The family joke was trying to figure out who had handed this genetic trait down to us, since neither of my parents could play basketball themselves. My brothers Fred and Frank were All-County and All-State in High School, with Frank being a top scorer in 1958. My sister Janice was a semi-pro basketball player in the industrial leagues. Despite my vision, and to the wonderment of Dr. Chandler, I was a good player too. Often in pick-up games, Frank and I weren't allowed to play on the same team because if we did, the other team didn't stand a chance.

My dreams of a basketball career, however, were cut short. My downfall came when gyms switched from solid white backboards to glass ones. I would shoot the ball using the white backboard as a guide, and aim toward the center. When they went to glass backboards, I couldn't see where to shoot at all.

Like sports, school would present its own challenges and difficulties. Because of my surgeries, I began my school career a little late. My eyesight put me in-between two worlds—not sighted enough to do well in regular school, but not impaired enough to be enrolled in a school for the blind. I was placed at a severe disadvantage, but also supported by my mother's belief that failure only comes from not trying.

I started in the first grade when I was eight years old, but then was skipped to the third grade because of my ability and age. However, because of my poor vision, through each grade I needed to rely on the empathy, flexibility, and helpfulness of my teachers. As I got older, though, and school became more difficult, I would try to compensate for my frustrations and insecurities with either class clown humor or explosive bursts of anger.

In school, as in daily life, what most people took for granted, I had to overcome. Getting from class to class was difficult in the dimly lit hallways. Reading from the chalkboard was impossible. Reading textbooks, I would have to put my face down against the page and read across, which slowed me down so much that I couldn't keep up with the other students. Instead of requiring me to copy down notes, some of my teachers would say, "I'll just test you on what you hear." Since I mostly had to rely on what I heard, rather than saw, I was encouraged to come up with my own set of problem-solving skills, especially in math, where I would devise my own equations. They usually worked. Most of my early teachers were sympathetic.

I did a lot of things that other kids did, but there was no doubt that my problems with sight resulted in some limitations. Because of this, I always had a lot of pent-up energy. All boys get into some mischief, but maybe I got into more than most:

Every morning in front of the school, we recited the *Pledge of Allegiance,* led by the principal, a former marine, with a drill instructor attitude. Just before the *Pledge* began, the flag was ready to be raised slowly up the pole. Nobody noticed that I had sneaked around to the highest platform with the rope in my hand. Suddenly, there was a Tarzan call, and the reverence was broken as I swung past the principal who had turned enough that my foot caught his hat as I sailed past, knocking it out of his hand. I misjudged the arc of the swing and almost went through the windows on the other side. I managed to stop myself in time, slamming into the wall instead, causing me to look more like George of the Jungle than Tarzan. There were screams and laughter.

"Richard, I'm going to be calling your parents!" I spent the day in the principal's office until Mom came over.

"Richard," she said angrily, "I swear to God, I don't know what I'm going to do with you!"

The principal agreed not to expel me, but throughout the course of the next five weeks, I had to do five thousand pushups (two hundred a day) and duck-walk two hundred times around the perimeter of the school—a typical military punishment.

When I was around fourteen or fifteen, my friend Tommy and I wanted something fun to do on the last day of summer before school, so we went to Rock Lake Pool. It was the end of summer and everyone was looking for his or her last fling.

It was the week before school, but inside the gate to the pool it was still summer. Little kids were running, splashing, and playing, and people were screaming down slides.

"Ladies and gentlemen, boys and girls," a voice boomed over a loudspeaker. "May I direct your attention to the top of the cliff. Rock Lake Pool proudly gives you the kamikaze high diving of the Great Carboni. Drum roll, please!" A guy with a snare drum began his quick beat. Everyone in the pool stopped splashing and hustled to get out of the way. The body builders stopped flexing, and the bikini girls stopped watching them. The pool was silent except for the drum.

The Great Carboni took off his cape and let it fall. He spread his arms and did deep knee bends, while the suspense built. Then he paused at the cliff's edge, struck a pose for the cameras, and dove into the pool. A wave of screams and applause hailed the Great Carboni as he reappeared above the water, and an admiring crowd gathered around him as he waded out of the pool to take his place of honor on the club house verandah.

"That's it?" Tommy said. "My dog could have done that, and he's dead."

"Is that so?" said a voice behind us. We turned to find the owner of the pool, who had thrown me out the week before for running down the big slide. "Mr. Turley, I thought I suspended you from the pool until next year."

"Your ticket man let us in."

"He was being generous because we had a show today, but if you two don't appreciate it, then you can leave now."

"C'mon," said Tommy, "tomorrow's Labor Day and then we're back at school."

"No chance," said the owner. "Now get, or I'll have you taken out!"

"But we already paid," I said.

"Well, that'll cover seeing the show you didn't like. Now, both of you get out. And don't come back tomorrow."

We headed out the gate and through the tunnel. "This is bullshit," I said. "We're going to get even with that old bastard."

"How?"

"By getting our money's worth. Just follow me," I replied.

We worked our way around the outside and walked up the train tracks past a sign that read "NO TRESPASSING." We began climbing up a steep path past a sign that said "NO CLIMBING." At the top of the path and through some bushes, we found ourselves on the high cliff above the pool. At the edge of the cliff lay the Great Carboni's cape.

"You're not gonna jump, are you?" asked Tommy.

"No, I'm gonna dive. If that guy and your dead dog can do it, so can I! Are you with me?"

Tommy laughed and looked over the edge. "Nah, I'll jump, but I ain't diving."

"Just tell me when the bottom is clear and when everyone is looking," I said.

Tommy cupped his hands around his mouth and began to yell down to the pool. "Hey, everyone! Up here! Up here!" Slowly I heard the place go quiet.

"Ladies and gentlemen, boys and girls!" Tommy shouted at the top of his voice. "I give you the Great Richard Turley! Drum roll please."

Tommy began a drum roll with his voice, and before I lost my nerve I stepped to the edge of the cliff, did a wave of my arms and a deep knee bend, waited for Tommy to say clear, and then I dove into the pool. The crowd in the pool erupted into applause and laughter. I swam a little and waited for Tommy to jump before wading out of the pool. Everyone was smiling and laughing, except the Great Carboni, who came down off the verandah glaring at me and stalked past. If looks could kill—

Tommy came running up with a big smile and the Great Carboni's cape. "Here superman, you forgot this."

Just behind him was the pool owner. My summer was over, but it was worth it.

"Now, Richard," I could already hear my mom saying when she found out, "you cut that foolishness out!"

For good or ill, I definitely stuck out, if not for the special attention that I needed (or attracted), then for my physical size. My brothers and I were tall. By my mid-teens I was six feet four inches and weighed two hundred pounds, which brought about another problem.

For young guys in Charleston during those days, there was a "king of the hill" mentality. If you had an issue with someone, or if you wanted recognition or respect, it meant getting into a fight. Usually it was started by smaller guys who always seemed to have something to prove, or maybe by someone with a brick sized chip on his shoulder. Other times fights began over a girl; sometimes it was just the simple need to show who was toughest. Some of the fights arose out of plain old prejudice and the need to keep some people "in their place." If challenged, you needed to stand up for yourself or else you would lose face. Because of my size and status as "the big man on campus," the athlete, the big flirt with all of the girls, and the joker, I often found myself in this position, and because of my fearlessness, I never flinched or backed down.

"Hey Richard, there's some guy across the street leaning against Mrs. William's store, and he wants to talk to you. I think he's looking for a fight."

"Oh God, not another one."

I walked across the street and said to the guy, "I understand you're looking for me."

"Sure am."

This kid was a lot smaller than I was, and I managed to talk him out of fighting me by reasoning with him that he would undoubtedly get hurt.

During my first year of high school, a bunch of guys were putting out the word that they were going to "sucker punch" any sophomores who were more than six feet tall. I didn't want to be sucker punched in one of the school's dark hallways, so I decided to be proactive and take them on out in the open. I found them during lunchtime at the Black Eagle. The Black Eagle's jukebox was playing when I walked in, so I went straight for it and pulled its plug from the wall. As the music died, the room became silent, except for one voice that yelled, "What the hell's going on?"

"I'm Richard Turley," I yelled back. "I'm a sophomore, I'm six foot-two, and I think you might be looking for me!"

I heard a couple of "you SOB," and other curses as they closed in on me. I swung first, like Dad taught me, but I was no match for that many fighters. I was still on my feet and had gotten five or six good punches in, but had been hit about ten times during the time it took for someone to run down the street and let my brother know what was happening.

Within moments Guy and my brother Frank, along with six seniors who were star football players, came through the door of the Black Eagle to break it up. The Turleys were clannish and fighters, so in these situations I was rarely alone. A problem with one Turley became a problem with them all, especially with my cousin Guy. Guy was a little older than I was at the time and he was tough, strong, good-looking, and the hardest hitter I had ever known. He could also be very funny and great to be around, especially in tight situations like the one I had just charged into.

I was a kind and big-hearted kid, but I could also be mean and ornery when the situation called for it. I knew that some kids called me "the one-eyed bastard" behind my back. But I had respect and, because I liked to take after my mom, I often tried to extend that respect in order to help or shield others. I hated (and still hate) bullies with a passion, and whenever someone who was a true underdog was being taken advantage of, I stepped in. I usually invited the bully to try me on for size instead. Sometimes they did, but it often didn't end well for the bully.

For most teenagers, school is their social universe—a place to meet and be with friends. Some relationships begin there and last a lifetime. The year before my Black Eagle incident, on the first day of the ninth grade, I met someone who became one of my best lifetime friends.

Ninth grade was the final year of what was still called Junior High School. I walked from home that morning, having forgotten what was going to make this first day of school different from all of the others. When I reached school, there was a big crowd standing around in a semicircle, but it was very quiet. I wondered what the hell was going on, and started to weave my way to the front of the crowd. Standing in the middle of the semicircle with their backs against a white-washed wall were nine black kids, being stared at like they were in a fish tank. This was a historic day—segregation (in the schools at least) had ended in South Charleston.

As I walked closer, I realized that these kids were scared. I walked down the line, extending my hand to each and introducing myself.

"Hi," I said, "my name's Richard Turley."

"One of the kids said in a low, deep voice, "I'm Jim Bruer."

"Wow, you've got a deep voice! Do you sing?"

Jim almost said, "yes sir," but he stopped himself and just said, "Yeah, I do."

"I sing and play guitar; we'll have to get together and sing sometime."

Scanning over the staring crowd, my protective instinct kicked in. As I shook Jim Bruer's hand again, I half-turned toward the crowd, and said to the new kids, "If any of you all need anything, come to me. If anyone bothers any of you, come tell me and I'll take care of it."

After that, the atmosphere loosened up. Friends began to talk, and the crowd spread out down the sidewalk and across the street. Some kids started to wait by the school door. It had become a nearly-normal day.

When we were called inside, everyone was directed to the auditorium for the opening of the year assembly. The black kids were given their own spot in the auditorium; old thinking dies hard, but I went and sat with them.

The Dean of Boys immediately came over and asked me if I'd rather sit in another part of the stands.

"No thanks," I said, "I'm fine."

He looked down at me and said, "I don't know why we put up with you," and then walked away.

I've never been prejudiced. I'm sure my mother had something to do with this.

Afterward, Jim Bruer told me that my gesture meant a lot to him and the other kids, and that it made things easier for them during those first uncertain weeks. I was glad to have helped and, more importantly, I had made a good friend.

Jim and I got together as I had suggested and started singing. Jim brought some more of his friends along, and we formed a singing group. Along with Jim Bruer, who was a natural bass singer, we got James Leaper, Homer Bayliss, Lonnie Spiller, and me. Dubbed "The Five Pearls," we sang R&B (rhythm and blues) and doo-wop (a style of vocal-based rhythm and blues) with harmony, energy, and soul. We sang at our school in the auditorium, and at the high school. Little did I know at the time that this group was the kickoff to my singing career.

CHAPTER 4

Music was my outlet and became my life by my freshman year. I could sing, I could play guitar, and it all came naturally, as if I were born to it. Music opened a new world to me, and it was a great time to be a teen in the world of music. Bill Haley, Elvis, and Jerry Lee Lewis had picked up the blues and had leaped with it into white mainstream.

By my sophomore year, school had become a different matter. I was becoming more and more frustrated, and I was getting into trouble more often than not. I hated the constant help and attention I needed. I was edgy and self-conscious, which was a bad combination. Luckily I had an outlet in music with the school chorus, which was an after-school activity. Unfortunately, after singing with the chorus only five or six times, I was asked to leave by the teacher. She took me aside, and said, "Sweetie, I know you've been to hell and back with all the surgeries, and it had to be extremely hard on you. Even though it pains me, I'm going to have to remove you from the chorus."

"What did I do?" I asked, thinking I was in trouble (go figure).

"You didn't do anything, Richard. You need to understand that you will never be a singer. One minute you're singing bass, and then baritone, and then tenor, and then alto, and for god sakes, even soprano. You're all over the place."

So I left the chorus. In later years, I was well known and revered within the music world for my freakish five-octave range. When I got my first advance from CBS/Columbia records for $25,000, I made a copy of it and sent it to her. Not very nice, I know but can you blame me?

My math teacher that same year always wrote the class tests on the board. She knew I couldn't see it, yet every time she made me ask her to give me the paper version. Then she would turn it into a big production, embarrassing me in front of my classmates. She would then turn to me, and in front of the class say, "Oh, I always have to do things special for you."

This was the fourth or fifth time she had called me out in front of the class, and this time I responded to her.

"But ma'am," I said, "It's not my fault that I can't see better. I'm just trying to make it through school."

She slapped her hands down on top of her desk, and spat out, "Well, maybe you would do better if you didn't play that rock 'n' roll."

I lost my temper and yelled, "You bitch!" as I overturned her desk, which ended up on top of her. I then turned to take myself to the Dean's office. I was so embarrassed that I had lost my temper. Mom and I had talked many times about Dad losing his temper, and I couldn't believe I was acting like Cody. Instead of calming down, though, I reacted again. On my way out of the room, I grabbed another desk and flung it through a window. I was sure glad no one was in that desk. I was suspended for ten days, at a time when I was going to need another eye surgery. The recovery time would have kept me out of school long enough that I would have been left back. No thanks I thought, so I had the surgery, and I dropped out of school at sixteen.

My father didn't have much to say either way about me dropping out. My mother, on the other hand, saw it as part of the inevitable course I would have to take. She knew that because of my lack of sight a "normal" career would never happen, and she saw music as my path. "You have talent," she would say, "You have to follow it."

I found that music and my friendships could take me to exceptional places, and I took advantage of every opportunity to play and sing. The black folks in South Charleston lived on certain parts of the Heights overlooking town, so we would say Jim Bruer lived "up on the hills." Jim, known as "Pete" or "Pete, Jr." to his family, belonged to the Vandalia Baptist Church, which balanced on the edge of a slope down the road from his house.

"Richard," he would say, "why don't you come up this Sunday? You can sing with us."

That was an invitation too good to refuse and ended up being everything I expected and hoped for. There was singing, shouting, and clapping in the aisles. Sometimes I would sing with some of the kids from the church in the alley behind school. Dinnertime would find them all sitting with me at "Mom Turley's" table eating good southern cooking, with fried chicken and biscuits on Sundays. My dad would be home to eat with us between shifts. It was a full house.

One night our "mixed race" dinners almost caused trouble. Mom was telling me that some of the neighbors were grumbling about having the black kids over to the house so much. Dad overheard the conversation, and came in saying, "What are you talking about?"

Mom replied, "It's nothing, Cody."

"No, you said people are grumbling. What are they grumbling about?"

My mom reluctantly gave in and told my dad that some of the neighbors were saying that they didn't like the fact that the black kids were at our house so much. They said that maybe the Turleys were turning into nigger lovers.

My dad looked out the window and saw five fathers standing around in the common yard. He said "Those guys out there?"

"Don't go out there, Cody."

"It's all right; I know what I'm doing."

"No Richard, you stay here."

I had gotten up to go with him because I was angry too.

My father walked up the alley on the side of our house and went into the backyard. My mom and I stood at the window and listened. The men from the neighborhood were talking and laughing, but when they saw my father, they fell silent. My dad got right to the point:

"I hear you guys been running your mouths and sayin' bad things about my family and calling my wife a 'nigger lover.' This is gonna stop and it's gonna stop right now!"

"Cody, we didn't say that! We didn't say anything at all."

"That's even worse if you're calling my wife a liar! I'll beat the hell out of you right now."

Nobody wanted to mess with Cody Turley, and not a one of them said a word.

My dad came home. "See? Nothing to worry about. I just don't want to hear it anymore, Silby. These are good kids. They pray at dinner, and now we do the same."

After I quit school I started forming bands. With classmate Donnie Carpenter and local guitarist Bob Garrett, we became Richard Turley and the Crystals, playing country-flavored rock, coined "Rock-a-Billy," and more R&B. From the Crystals we morphed into Richard Turley and the Travelers, which recruited more local talent like Butch Lester, Norman Chapman, Gary Hawks, and Eddie Seckman. We would rehearse in my garage with the door open, while the neighbors and kids hung around in the driveway and on the lawn. We worked out our own versions of "Long Tall Sally" and "Johnny B. Goode," the big hits of the time. The attention rocketed, and so did my ego.

The Kanawha valley was becoming the center of West Virginia's music scene, creating opportunities for local bands and artists. Charleston had the venues and the media, and whatever happened there spread to the smaller cities. Like us, American Rock was in its adolescence, and we had plenty of role models and idols. We had graduated from Bill Haley and Elvis to the super nova energy of Little Richard, the cool innocence of Buddy Holly, and the rocking hooks and lyrics of Chuck Berry. Roy Hamilton, Hank Ballard and the Midnighters, Clyde McPhatter, the Drifters, and Fats Domino—all of them created music we wanted to dance to. My band was hot, and we were going to be just as big.

The recognition was intoxicating and addictive. We played everywhere, from regional small bars and taverns to auditoriums and television shows in Charleston and throughout the state. Summers had gone from the basketball league to Saturday night music at the Shoney's Big Boy drive-in or the record hops at Rock Lake Pool.

Shoney's featured a radio disc jockey (DJ) named "Lonesome Larry." Just the name alone made me want to talk to him, and I'd go up to his booth to hang out and talk about music. It was "American Graffiti" in West Virginia.

If you were young in the Kanawha Valley in late '50s, the place to be was on The Dick Reid Record Hop. Reid was a former DJ in Charleston before landing his teen-oriented music show on WCHS, a local affiliate of CBS. He modeled his show after Dick Clark's *American Bandstand*.

In his mid-thirties with an easy manner and a suit and tie, he was our local celebrity. He had heard of Richard Turley and the Travelers and came to one of our shows.

Afterward he introduced himself saying, "Son, you're fantastic, you're going to go places. I would love to have you on the show."

We became a regular act on the *Record Hop*, playing three weeks each month. When Reid took us on his road show across the state, he tagged me "The West Virginia Superstar." The small town kids responded with hysteria, probably overcome with having honest-to-goodness TV stars playing in their towns and before their eyes (thanks, Elvis). We had to run for our lives figuratively from the screaming girls, and literally from their jealous boyfriends. Every week *The Record Hop* was like a school dance for the entire Valley.

The height for Reid came when Dick Clark brought his "Caravan of Stars" to Charleston, but it ended up creating one of the most embarrassing moments I had experienced in my sixteen years.

Reid was in great form, introducing Dick Clark to the screaming kids in the Charleston Auditorium and then Clark took over, smooth and full of charisma. We had won a battle of the bands contest to open the show for Fabian, Chubby Checker, Frankie Avalon, and Bobby Rydell. My band was hot, and when the excitement of the crowd swept over us we knew we had arrived. The next day it was all over the newspapers.

The Charleston Gazette: "We were so lucky last night at the Charleston Memorial Auditorium, where our beloved Dick Reid had the opportunity to introduce the world-famous Dick Clark. However, the show was stolen by our own Little Dick Turley . . ."

Imagine the teasing I endured over that one. I thought it would never end.

A couple of months later, I was playing in a show for Dick Reid in Logan, West Virginia, and the audience (of mostly girls) had gone insane. I was on stage with my band, taking in the girls' energy and giving it right back. My mom, bless her seamstress heart, had made me a gaudy Liberace-style jacket to perform in. Near the end of the show I stripped it off and threw it (partly out of excitement, and partly because I hated it), into the audience.

It was like feeding time at the alligator pit. A wild frenzy started, and my jacket was torn to shreds. It was a rock star's dream seeing all those girls fighting over a piece of clothing just because I had worn it. Unfortunately, however, the crowd turned briefly into a mob and went out of control. One girl wound up with a broken arm. I should have known better. A couple of months before, about fifty girls had overturned our car. After that, when we pulled up to a venue, I would have to sink down in the backseat to keep from being seen and capsized. Crazy to think about, and scary when it's happening, but this time I had fed the flames.

In the interest of virtue and public safety, the Mayor of Logan said that I wouldn't be allowed back. Dick Reid was furious, and made me write an apology to the local newspapers for having started all the trouble. I heard later that one of the girls proudly wore her trophy, one of my jacket sleeves, to school the next Monday. I had become a teen idol in West Virginia, and it was all fun, but I was serious about music and had higher goals. It was time to grow up and go up.

CHAPTER 5

I was seventeen, and like most people that age, I discovered I was outgrowing my roots. I knew that if I wanted to make a career in music, I was going to have to leave home. I had been encouraged, nourished, and protected, but it was time now to look beyond the Kanawha Valley.

Because of Dick Reid, I had notoriety outside of South Charleston, and that was how I met Don Hickson. Don was in his mid-thirties and had worked for Dot and Decca Records. He saw me perform in Charleston and thought I had a big career ahead of me, if I had the right manager. Don was a good guy who wanted to help me to the top. To show me around, he took me on my first trip to New York City. This would be just a look and learn trip, and we'd be back in South Charleston within a few days.

A few months before the trip I had what would be my final eye surgery with Dr. Chandler. The hope with each surgery was that my sight would improve.

This had been my routine since I was six. I would lie on his operating table and, fully awake, allow Dr. Chandler to remove cataract and scar tissue. Six needles would be inserted around my eye, three above and three beneath, with injections that would numb my face. My eye would then be carefully brought out onto my cheek. Dr. Chandler would go about his delicate work, while I watched as if looking the wrong way through binoculars. What to me looked like tiny hands with tiny scissors from far away, would slowly cut, while I talked and asked questions the entire time.

Exasperated, he would say, "Richard, shut up and don't move! I'm operating on your eye!"

To which I only replied, "Wow. I bet that hurts."

Bandaged, I would then wait, expecting with a child's excitement that when the bandages were removed I would be able to see the world as everyone else did. It never worked out that way. I thought maybe this time it would, but it wasn't meant to be.

A few months later, Don and I shared the ten-hour drive to and from New York. I wish I could have seen the famous Manhattan skyline from a distance, but I couldn't until it was literally on top of us as we came out of the Lincoln Tunnel.

New York was big, and I felt every inch the country boy. We checked into the Taft Hotel on 51st Street, near the famous Brill Building, just a few blocks up from Times Square. Don was hoping for fate to smile down on us, and it almost did. Staying at the Taft were Jackie Wilson, The Platters, and the Crickets, minus Buddy Holly. This was real excitement, and I managed to talk our way into a party they were throwing on the first floor. We had a great time, and Don made some good connections.

On the way home, we didn't have enough money to stop and sleep in a hotel, so we slept in the car. We parked in a rest stop along a lonely strip of the Pennsylvania Turnpike. For me, it was as dark as if we had parked in a cave. It was late spring so we were able to leave the windows open a little, letting in a cool breeze. Just another singer's night on the road, and because I was so tall, I got the backseat. I tried to sleep lying across the seats with my face looking up and out of the back window, but in the middle of the night I woke up, my legs and neck stiff from sleeping at odd angles.

With my eyes opening on the black sky, it took me a few moments to focus, and to remember where I was. Then I noticed something I had never seen before; the sky looked strange, like it was dotted with lights. Maybe my last surgery had helped, but maybe my sight was getting worse. I was suddenly worried.

"Don, wake up. Wake up, man!"

"What, what is it?"

"What the hell is that?"

"What the hell is what?"

"Those lights up there. Do you see them?"

"You mean those lights?" Don pointed at the sky.

"Yeah, you see them?"

"Of course I do."

I was relieved. I was excited. "What are they?" I asked.

"Richard, are you kidding me?"

"No, what are they?"

"They're called stars."

"Oh my God, really?! I've never seen stars before."

I was excited and sad at the same time. Excited that my eyesight might have gotten better, but sad to think about all I was missing.

"Mom!" I called into the house as I went up the stairs to the kitchen.

"Richard?" My Mother answered. "You're back already? Where's Don? Why didn't you invite him in?"

"Don just dropped me off. He wanted to get straight home to his wife. But Mom, there's something important I need to tell you. Just sit down. It's something I saw."

"In New York?"

"No, something last night, on the road. We had a great time in New York. When we left New York we were broke, so we had to sleep in the car last night. I was in the backseat looking up through the window. I couldn't sleep and I'm looking up and I see these lights up in the sky. Don had to tell me what they were. I thought my eyes were getting worse, but they weren't. They're getting better! I saw stars in the sky—stars, Mom."

"Oh my God," my mother sat down. "Maybe that last surgery worked." She started to cry, and then I started to cry with her.

Suddenly something caught my eye out the window, and I said "Mom, what's that out there?" I pointed out the window, "What are all those black things?"

Mom wiped her eyes and looked out the window. "Those are birds, Richard."

This started both of us crying again. I think that my mom had tried to keep hold of her faith all those years, but inevitably it had begun to falter as time went on. Now she saw a glimmer of hope. "Honey, maybe things are going to get better," she said. And they did get better, for a time.

Don Hixson arranged my first recording contract. I didn't have a contract with Don, but I told him that if he could get me a record deal, then I'd let him manage me. He came through, and in 1959, three months before my eighteenth birthday, I signed with Fraternity Records out of Cincinnati. Fraternity was a record label that distributed to the Ohio Valley, but eventually scored national chart hits with Cathy Carr, Jimmy Dorsey's Orchestra, Bobby Bare, and Lonnie Mack. It was a diverse label, running from bubble gum, country, and pop to the new sounds of rock 'n' roll and Rock-A-Billy.

Fraternity's founder and owner was Harry Carlson, who always seemed to wear the same gray suit. Carlson was very much the country charmer but he was also a businessman; he knew what he could sell and what he couldn't. Elvis Presley was the King of rock 'n' roll then and, to Carlson, I was going to be Fraternity's Elvis.

I told Mr. Carlson, "I do rhythm and blues and soul way better than I do Elvis music."

"Listen son," Carlson said to me in his big, "Foghorn Leghorn" voice. "You show me a white boy makin' hit records in R&B and Soul in the *Billboard* magazine, then I'll record you that way."

When he said it that way, I suddenly understood, so I looked at Mr. Carlson and gave my best Elvis impersonation complete with hip swivel saying, "Thank ya very much." Carlson laughed. He liked this kid Richard Turley from West Virginia, and he was going to make him one of his stars.

I was still only seventeen, so my mom had to sign the contract for me. It was a deal to record four songs with options for more at the discretion of Fraternity Records. It was a great deal for a kid making his first record, but to be honest, I was so young and eager, they could have put a napkin down in front of me and I would have signed it. I did learn my first important lesson in music: a new artist has no control. If the record label wants a certain style, that's what you have to give them or "no deal."

That winter I went down to Cincinnati's King Studios to make my first single. Fraternity wanted me but not my band, so I found myself working with studio musicians for the first time. My band was great on stage, but I immediately realized the difference between working with pros who knew how to work quickly, with originality and precision. Studio musicians know how to use the studio to create great music, and their talents can find that missing ingredient for any hit record. Think of the opening guitar on Chuck Berry's "Johnny B. Goode." A good hook can turn any record to gold.

We recorded both sides of my first 45, "All About Ann," a ballad, and "Makin' Love with My Baby," a Rock-a-Billy song. Both songs were originals, and "Makin' Love with My Baby" was recently inducted into the Rock-a-Billy Hall of Fame. Making the record, seeing my name on Fraternity's blue label of shooting stars, and finally hearing my voice come out of a radio gave me chills.

Fraternity was so pleased with the record that they booked studio time to make a follow-up. This time, Harry Carlson wanted to shoot for Elvis's more sophisticated, crooner style. The recordings would be done in Nashville, with more orchestrated arrangements, at the Bradley's Barn studio founded by the famed Owen Bradley. Bradley had already recorded some of country music's biggest stars, and had branched out to work with rockers like Buddy Holly and Gene Vincent.

Despite all of this music history and prestige, my only reaction when we pulled up to the studio was, "Damn! It looks like a barn!"

Once inside the studio, however, I saw and heard what the Barn, and the famous Nashville Sound, was all about.

We were booked to record two songs: "When I'm Alone" and "Since I Met You," with the cream of Nashville's session players. We had the Anita Kerr singers, Floyd Cramer, Hank

Garland, Grady Martin, and fellow West Virginian Charlie McCoy, plus Elvis's bass player, Bob Moore, and drummer Buddy Harmon, Another record and another ego boost for me. It was time to take another step up the ladder, and Don Hixson would lead the way. In the meantime, I continued to play with the band around the region.

"Promotional photo of Richard Turley for Fraternity Records, 1959."

In the fall of 1959, I was playing at the Twin Maples Tavern in St. Albans, when the band was approached during a break by a bar owner. He said he loved the way we sounded, and wanted us to play for him. I found out his club was between Hurricane and Barboursville, which was pretty far for us to travel. I didn't think any of our crowd would come that far out, but the owner insisted he had more than 150 customers every weekend night. He said we could play for the door, so we would earn a dollar a head. It sounded like a good deal, and we agreed.

Three weeks later, we made the drive, unloaded our gear, and headed in. A couple of rummy looking guys were sitting at the bar. The owner came out to meet us.

"Where's the crowd?" we asked.

"Don't worry, they'll be in."

"You sure?" I glanced over at the regulars, not convinced.

"Don't worry, you guys set up and start playing. You'll see."

We played a set and then took a break. An hour went by, we played a couple more songs, and still no crowd. The guys at the bar didn't move. Maybe they couldn't. One of our "audience" was now face down on the bar.

"Hey man, what the hell is this? You said you got 150 people every night."

"Well, you guys had such a big crowd in St. Albans, I figured they'd follow you out here."

"What? Why in the hell would anyone come all the way out here? We're not even sure where we are. You were just lying, and you wasted our time!"

"Well, guys, I don't know what to say, you might as well pack up. Since there was no door, I can't pay you anything."

The band was pissed, but what could we do? We started packing up and taking everything to the cars. On the first trip out I noticed that the club had a big, ornate front door, and I got an idea. When we finished loading up, I got a screw driver from one of the station wagons.

"Where are you going with that?" one of the guys asked.

"Just watch," I said, "I'm gonna get even with this guy."

I swung the front door open and started to unscrew it from the hinges. After I got the first hinge loose the owner finally noticed me and came running over from the bar.

"What the hell are you doing?!" he yelled.

"I'm getting paid, that's what." I started removing the bottom hinge.

"What?"

"You said that we could play for the door. Well, we played, so now I'm taking what we earned."

"You son of a bitch. That door cost me $500, Now, get the hell out of here!"

I stood up and faced him. "Mister," I said, "I could kick your ass, and your bartender's ass at the same time. Now, you've got a choice. Pay us fifty dollars and I'll leave, or I'm taking the damn door!"

He cursed something under his breath, and I'm not sure whether it was directed at us, the door, the evening, or rock 'n' roll in general. It didn't matter though, because he quickly came back with the fifty bucks. He handed me the money, and I handed him the screws.

I passed the bills out to each of the guys and, laughing, we hopped into the station wagons and drove off. The owner yelled after us that we'd never play there again. No problem, friend! A wasted night, but the story was pure gold. For years afterward in West Virginia, it was well known that Richard Turley played for the door.

A couple of months after we left Nashville, Don contacted one of his old friends from Decca Records, Tom Simms, who was now working promotions in Pittsburgh for DOT records. Originally founded in Tennessee, DOT itself was based in Hollywood and carried an artist list ranging from Count Basie and Pat Boone to Jimmie Rodgers. Don told his friend about me, and Simms said they were interested and asked Don to send a demo and a photograph.

Instead of an audition, Don sent my Nashville recordings to Tom Simms. When Simms called back, he said that the DOT people had loved the two songs and wanted to sign me. An agreement was reached, and Harry Carlson sold my contract to DOT. To me, it was like being sold out of the minor leagues to play for the Yankees. DOT wasn't just a record company, but was also owned by Paramount Pictures. They loved my record and the big time was calling. The West Virginia Superstar was going national. All my drive and talent was going to pay off, and I was sure I was going to be rich and famous. It didn't happen because DOT never promoted me. Tom Simms wouldn't return our calls, and the record disappeared.

"What the hell happened?" I asked Don.

"We'll probably never know," he said. "All I can say for sure is 'that's the record business.' Hot one minute, not the next."

I later learned that big record companies like DOT bought up the contracts of smaller labels like Fraternity to keep down the competition. Whatever the real reason, I learned my second big lesson in music. Promotion and power are more important than talent. DOT had decided to move on, and with no agreement to record me, I was left behind.

Don Hixson also decided to move on. Don was on his second marriage and had decided to move back to his new wife's home in Peoria, Illinois, where they opened a dance studio together. I was on my own, and I needed to make a move too. If DOT Records was in Los Angeles, then that's where I was going. If I could just talk to the people there, then they'd promote my record and sign me to make more. They just needed to meet me, and everything would fall into place. Doesn't that sound like an eighteen-year-old?!

Joining me were three local musicians: Austin Parsons on bass, Jim Angel on drums, and Gary Hawks on piano. We were united by a desire to make music and to make it big, and all three jumped at the chance to go with me. My eldest sister Janice and my brother Fred had already moved to California. Both had settled in Los Angeles, Janice in Pacific Palisades with her retired Air Force husband, and Fred in Englewood with a good job as a comptroller. All Los Angeles needed now was to hear Richard Turley.

With my own money I bought an old Ford station wagon with wood paneling on the sides and an annoying squeak as we rode down the highway. Jim told us to call him when we had everything lined up and he and Austin would follow us out. So, packed in with our gear and Jim's drum kit, Gary and I left South Charleston in the winter of 1960 full of hopes and dreams. Obviously I couldn't help drive, and I couldn't see much as we crossed the plains and the Southwest, living on soda and sandwiches and sleeping in ten-dollar-a-night motels. I knew we had left winter behind when we reached Los Angeles, though, because the weather was perfect.

After we got set up in a hacienda motel, I went to DOT Records to introduce myself, generate some interest, and maybe get another chance to record. It turned out they were no more interested in Richard Turley standing in their lobby than they were when he was two thousand miles away in West Virginia.

After introducing myself to the receptionist, who took my name and called the executive offices, I waited confidently for the message to "send Mr. Turley up." After all, I was one of their recording artists. I imagined the president of DOT, Randy Wood, coming out of his office to personally introduce himself. So I stood, sat, walked around, and watched people come and go. No call.

I talked to the receptionist again, who said that someone should be coming down soon. More standing, and waiting, but nothing happened and the whole day had gone by. I spoke to the receptionist one more time.

"I'm sorry," she said, "but I don't think anyone's coming down. I don't know what happened. Can I take your number where someone can call you?"

"No thanks," I said.

DOT turned out to be a locked door, and to make matters worse, Los Angeles wasn't the paradise of opportunity I had imagined. Musically, I had landed on barren land. Los Angeles was a movie town, and few venues had anything resembling a stage for bands to perform on. LA wasn't the music hub it would be later in the sixties with the advent of the Byrds, the Beach Boys, and other California groups. Even the clubs owners we auditioned for, who were willing to hire us, weren't willing to pay. Instead they offered the old "you can play for the door" routine, but I had seen the doors in LA, and they weren't as ornate as the one in West Virginia, so we passed.

A couple of weeks later, we heard that Austin Parsons had died in a car accident back in West Virginia, a tragedy for his family, for us, and for all of his friends back home. Now it was going to be just the two of us until Jim flew out. When I realized the seriousness of my situation, in a sprawling and indifferent city so far from home, I was very discouraged, but at least I had Janice and Fred to fall back on.

Gary didn't know anyone else in California, so he got a day job. With him working, we didn't have the time to perform even if we found a place to play. With nothing lined up musically, Jim wasn't coming out. Disgusted with the outcome all the way around, I sold the car, my guitar, and amps. I had Jim's drum kit shipped back to Charleston, and moved in with my brother Fred. I thought it was over.

Unfortunately my options were as limited as my vision. I tried taking a class at a vocational college, but I just couldn't see well enough to do it. I also couldn't see well enough to hold down a regular job. Instead I would spend my time working out at the gym, shooting pool, and picking up girls. I was also wearing out my welcome at Fred's, so after three months, I decided it was time to swallow my pride and go back home. Janice and Fred saw me off at the train station where Fred shook my hand while Janice cried. I was still only eighteen, but this was my first experience with failure, and I had a long trip ahead of me to think about what I was going to do next.

For awhile I was able to forget the previous three months, but when the train was within fifty miles of South Charleston I started to wonder how my family and friends were going to react to seeing me, and how I was going to react to them. I had always been tough, but now I didn't feel tough, and I hoped that only Mom and Dad would be at the station. When we pulled in, my mom and dad were waiting on the platform. Cody didn't say much when I stepped off the train, so it was my mom who first noticed that I didn't have my guitar with me.

"Where's your guitar?" she asked.

"I sold it, Mom," I answered irritably. I was angry at Los Angeles, angry at DOT Records, and angry at the whole business. "I'm done with music."

"But you can't be!"

"I am," I said, and I meant it.

CHAPTER 6

"I'm done with music," I said disgustedly.

"But you can't be," my mom replied. "You can't quit just like that."

"Yes I can," I said, and then I told her all that had gone wrong in California.

I kicked around South Charleston for a while, hung around with some friends, and played basketball. I heard Gary Hawks had come home, but I didn't go see him because the bad taste of Los Angeles was still too fresh. Music wasn't on my mind, and I had nothing to play with anyway, since I had sold my guitar. I didn't realize how upset my mother was with me until about a month after I came home from Los Angeles.

One afternoon I went down into the basement and there in the middle of the floor was a new electric guitar and amp.

"Mom! What is this?" I yelled.

My mom came down the stairs. "What's what?" she asked innocently with a sly little smile.

"That," I pointed at the new guitar.

"Well, it looks like a guitar and amp to me."

"And where'd it come from?"

"I got it for you from Herbert's Music. Mr. Herbert helped me and said it was a good one and just what you needed."

"I told you, Mom, I'm done with music."

"And like I told you, you can't be. You have a gift and a talent, and everyone says you're really great. You can't just quit."

"How did you pay for it?" I asked.

"That doesn't matter," my mom answered.

"Well, if you won't tell me, then I'm taking it right back to Herbert's."

"And I'll just buy you another one."

"And I'll take it right back!" I said a little louder.

"And I'll buy another," she said a little louder.

"And I'll take it *back!*" I said even louder.

"And I'll buy *another.*"

"And I'll—"

I stopped in mid-sentence and we just stared at each other. We broke down laughing and hugged. When two Turley's fought, the best we could hope for was a draw.

"Honey," my mom said, "everybody says that you're the best singer they've ever heard. God gave you a gift, and you've got to use it. I taught you to never give up and defeat is no option. I knew you needed to be stronger and more determined than most. Honey, we don't know what's going to happen with your eyes. You might be totally blind someday, and music is how you're going to earn your living. You need your music, and you can't just quit."

We hugged again, and I realized how much my music meant to her, and how much she loved me. There was no one I loved more than my mother, and I refused to let her down. I was back in the music business.

Two or three months later, I was contacted by an R&B band that I had met a year earlier while recording in Cincinnati. They asked me to join them for a gig in Alabama because their lead singer quit on them and they needed a quick replacement. It was an all-black group who loved my R&B/soul singing and, just as importantly, knew that I didn't have a prejudiced bone in my body. We were singers and musicians who loved R&B, and that's all that mattered.

The gig was at Maxwell Air Force Base in Montgomery, Alabama, and so in two station wagons filled with our equipment we drove into the heart of the old south. Did I think twice about this? Not at all. Was I naïve about where we were headed? Maybe. We were an integrated band performing in a state where a lot of people still thought the Civil War had never ended. Besides, it was an Air Force base, where blacks and whites served together. We'd be safe—and sure enough, the crowd loved us.

"You guys are great," a white officer said to us after the show. "You know, there's a music club in town that'll love to have you. You should check it out."

The officer gave us the name of the place, and after we packed up our gear we went down to the club. The officer was right—they wanted us to play and booked us for the following night. The next night we set up, the regulars filed in, and soon the house was filled with an all-white crowd eager to hear some hot rhythm and blues.

The band played alone for the first twenty minutes with the excitement building and I was standing just off stage, ready to make a dramatic entrance.

"Now everybody," one of the guys in the band, yelled to the crowd, "please welcome Mr. Dynamite himself—Richard Turley!"

Whoops and applause, and I ran out on stage. When the screaming crowd saw me they stopped dancing and applauding, and the room felt ice cold. The crowd whispered to each other, some pointing at the stage.

We played a couple of songs and still got no reaction, but when we took a break, the rest of the band went out back for a smoke. I slid down the front of the stage, hoping to warm up some of the crowd by talking to them. Three guys came up to talk to me:

"We got one question for you," one of them said. "What the hell are you doing singing with these niggers?"

Since I was a kid, nothing ever scared me and, as usual, I tried to turn on the Richard Turley charm and make a joke.

"Well," I said, "they let me sing with them if I shine their shoes and keep their pants pressed,"—just a little sarcasm, which probably pissed them off more.

"We think every nigger should be hung."

"Well, I hear three of the guys are hung to their knees."

"This ain't funny," one of them said. "You're gonna be sorry," said another, and they turned and walked back into the crowd.

Oh shit.

I found the guys in the band out back, and told them what happened. We went back on stage to start playing again and about halfway through the first song, with the band kicking ass, I heard a loud pop. Holy shit! It was gunfire and we were being shot at! I was told the first bullet whizzed past my head and hit the wall behind us. The other guys knew I was the target and they pushed me down to the floor to cover me while they took out their own guns. I had been a little naïve about the trip, but the guys in the band weren't, and they had come armed. Holy Shit!!!

The shots continued, but either they were all lousy shots, or they were really drunk because nobody was getting hit. The place cleared out to the sounds of screams and shuffles and cracking furniture.

"C'mon, Richard!" The guys hustled me outside and threw me into the back of one of the station wagons. "Stay down!" They yelled.

They went back inside to grab their equipment and off we went, still under fire, as we hauled ass out of the parking lot.

When we got back to Cincinnati, the drummer of the band, Frankie Simmons, loved to tell everyone what happened, and he could do it without taking a breath.

"You know, Richard was up there singing, man," Frank would start, "and all of sudden POW! there was gunfire, man, and we knew god damn it these guys was gonna kill us—these five niggers and this nigger lover—and we knew we had to get Richard out of there and we got him in the back seat and we got our stuff and we were firing back at them and they were firing back at us and we got our equipment in the car and we took off then and we drove until we got across the Alabama border and I stopped the car and jumped up on the hood and I called them a whole *baaagggg* of motherfuckers!"

"A whole bag of motherfuckers." Frankie had summed it up pretty well.

I never told my mom what had happened. What would be the point? If I had, she would have summed it up in her own special way, "Now, Richard," she would have said, "you cut that foolishness out." Amen, Mom.

I was lucky to be alive. We all were. But if it was all foolish then, I certainly didn't learn my lesson because the following year I wound up taking part in one of the first Freedom Ride marches down in Jackson, Mississippi. Fifty years later, I still can't recall exactly how I ended up with four white college guys who were going to Jackson to join the March. They were all a little older than I was and looking back, they may have wanted me to come along, not so much because of my dislike of racism but for my size. Personally, I believed in what the Freedom Riders were trying to accomplish, and since I couldn't integrate Rock Lake Pool, I was going to get even by integrating the whole damn country.

We drove down to Jackson and found the March already underway. There must have been thousands of people, both black and white, in the streets, along with hundreds of cops, FBI agents, and National Guard. The city was expecting trouble, but who was going to start it? The marchers or the people they were marching against?

We learned the answer when we turned a corner and walked into a line of about thirty Ku Klux Klansmen, all dressed in their white sheets and hoods. They were carrying crow bars and baseball bats, and they were looking to break heads—our heads. "Nigger-lovers!" they shouted at us, and we turned and ran, not knowing we were headed down a dead end street. Trapped, we had no choice but to turn and face them. This was different from any of the fights that I had ever experienced back home. None of that "king of the hill" crap here—this was about survival, and I thought for sure we were going to be beaten to death. "Nigger-lovers, nigger-lovers, nigger-lovers!" came their chant.

Just as I braced myself for the inevitable, two cars screeched up in front of us. Out of one car came the sheriff, and piling out of the other was a group of FBI agents. The cavalry had arrived just in time, and they had stopped the Klan from getting to us. Just as we started to relax, the Sheriff walked over to our side of the street.

"Look you nigger-lovers, you get the fuck out of my town, and if you ever come back here, I'll shoot you myself!"

At that, the Klansmen resumed their chant.

One of the FBI guys walked over to the sheriff and told him not to say stuff like that to us because it was all on record.

"I don't care what you got on record," the sheriff said to him. "You just take these god-damned assholes out of here."

The chanting around us continued.

We were put into the FBI's station wagon and taken out of town and back to our car. More than three hundred people were arrested that day, most of them Freedom Riders. Driving back to West Virginia, we knew we were lucky to be alive. For me, it pretty much ended my career as an activist, but in my personal and professional life I knew I could still make a difference, even in a small way. By the late sixties I wanted to start making a difference through my songs, so I wrote "Freedom Mountain."

Come on children black and white,
We've got to get together and do what's right,
We've got to stand side by side,
And build this mountain up to the sky . . .
We've got to build this mountain for freedom.[2] (Richards 1968)

I put together a new band with Jim Angel, which began a lifelong friendship. Two local guys, Bill Holden on piano and Butch Lester on bass, rounded us out. Bill's nickname was "Flash" because he was so reserved and quiet. Butch Lester was from St. Alban's and was a dyed-in-the-wool country boy. Together, we were a really good band.

My vision had improved with the last surgery, and Dr. Chandler sent me to an optometrist who fitted me with a contact lens. Every teenager wants a driver's license, and now I was twenty, so I decided I had waited long enough. I still needed special clearance from Dr. Chandler for the license because my vision was only 20/70. It would be a hard sell. The license would be for "day-time driving" only but even so, Dr. Chandler was reluctant to sign for me. Unfortunately for him I was a real pain in the ass, and wouldn't take "no" for an answer. Eventually he relented and I got my license. Look out West Virginia! Make way for Richard Turley, (at least between dawn and dusk).

Throughout the years, when people find out I used to drive, they tend to ask me if I ever had a wreck. I always reply in my best Mr. Magoo voice, "No, but I saw seventeen in my rear-view mirror!"

Getting my new band off the ground might take some time, and I needed to pay the bills, so with my new driver's license I decided to land a day job. I was a big kid with a big personality, and as Dr. Chandler could attest, I could sell anything. Those were the days when travelling salesman went door to door, and I worked for two companies. First was the Fuller Brush company, and then was the Family Record Plan, an outfit that would take baby photos and then offer a plan to take more throughout the years as the kids grew up. I did well, becoming one of the company's top earners, but it was just temporary. Music was my goal,

---

[2] *Freedom Mountain,* Turley Richards, Ridge Music, Warner Brothers Music, BMI, 1968

and an opportunity soon came to me from an old acquaintance, Randy Jay, who was a disc jockey and program director for radio station WCEF in Parkersburg.

Parkersburg is West Virginia's third largest city, and Randy Jay would become one of the bigger names in West Virginia radio. Jay, whose real name was Calvin Daily, was a smart go-getter just a few years older than I was. He answered a WCEF help-wanted ad for a DJ straight out of high school, landed the job, and eventually moved up to program director, then general manager, and finally became the owner of WCEF as well as several other radio stations around the State. In 1959 he had heard about Richard Turley, Dick Reid's West Virginia Superstar, and booked me to come up to Parkersburg for a couple of shows. In late 1961 and early 1962, he had me come back for a couple of gigs on the weekends when I wasn't working my other job. The trips to Parkersburg were always fun, and I was able to meet some other club owners who began to book me.

In 1963, I went back to Parkersburg with Jim Angel, and Rueben Seegars. Rueben was an excellent organist who played a B3 organ, which enabled him to kick the baseline with his foot. The end result was we had one less player to pay.

In the nightclubs I was able to do more jazz, which was fine with me since, musically, jazz was my first love. The Red Fox didn't work out but at the Wheel things took off, becoming a four- or five-night commitment. So in early '63 Parkersburg became my home away from home.

Jim Angel and I briefly roomed together. Jim was having a good time and could always make us laugh with his non-stop talk. Jim's personality was so big he could talk the pants right off of any woman. The only problem was, he never knew when to shut up and would miss the opportunity and talk their pants right back on. Eventually, when I could afford it, I moved into my own little room.

I was having a good time in Parkersburg and making decent money at the club, but the better part of my income wasn't coming from music. I played a mean game of pool, and in town was a place called the Castle that stayed open past midnight to cater to the all-night crowd. The Castle had several pool tables, so after the Wheel closed for the night, most of us headed over there to relax over a two AM breakfast, where I would sometimes play pool for the rest of the night. I often played for money, and in a good week I could make between $400 and $500 just at the pool table, which was quite a bit more than the $175 I was making at the Wheel. I always watched the other guy play for a while to size him up, just as I had seen Paul Newman do in *The Hustler*. One night it paid off.

Parkersburg had its share of colorful characters passing through, and one night I watched a guy from Philadelphia beat a local at pool to the tune of $700. After the local backed out, the guy from Philly turned to the room and announced, "Okay, any more of you hillbillies want to try me? I'll take any of yooz' one-handed." The guy was a real smart-ass; he had a big guy sitting by the door as though he was supposed to be a bodyguard. No one spoke up—no one except me, of course. I had intently watched him play and decided that he was a lot better than I was, but I didn't like this guy, and I had a con in mind.

"I'll take you on," I said, "but I've got a better idea. Instead of you playing with one hand, how about we both play with only one eye?"

"How's that gonna work?"

"We both blind fold one of our eyes, and then we play."

The guy thought for a moment. "Okay, kid, you're on."

We rigged up patches over our eyes and began to play.

Of course, he didn't know I only had one eye, and while he was adjusting to his new but temporary condition, I won every game and took him for $800.

Finally he'd had enough. "This is bull-shit. Let's play without the stupid, fucking patch."

But like any good hustler, I knew to quit while I was ahead. "No thanks," I said, trying to soften the mood. "I saw how good you are, and you'll beat the hell out of me."

The guy looked around the room, then said to his goon, "Aaah, forget it! Let's get the fuck out of this one-horse town." As they left the Castle, we all laughed. After he was gone, I gave $650 of my winnings back to the local to replace the $700 he lost.

The year 1963 was starting to slip by, and I was hoping for some new opportunities. We were at the Continental Club across the river in Belpre, playing more jazz. It was an upscale restaurant, so I had to wear a tuxedo (which didn't hurt me with attracting the ladies).

"Well," I joked to Jim and Reuben, "at least we finally made it out of West Virginia."

I knew I couldn't do this much longer, and I started thinking about my quick trip to New York with Don Hixson where I got to hang out with the Platters, the Crickets, and Jackie Wilson. If I was going to have a real career in music, I had to go east not west this time.

In LA I'd had Fred and Janice to fall back on, but I didn't know anyone in New York. The only Turley to ever try and make it in New York City was my sister Carolyn, who travelled there to become an actress. She lasted all of one day before, totally overwhelmed and intimidated, she returned home. That was not going to happen to me, so going to New York would require some solid contacts or a lot of money. I didn't have the contacts, so my plan was to raise a thousand dollars and then go.

Then opportunity knocked.

One night I was on stage at the Continental when I spotted two glamorously dressed women sitting together right in front of the stage. I smiled at them, and during a break they waved me over. Good looking socialites in their late-thirties, they gave the impression of two wealthy and sophisticated women out on the town.

"Come and sit between us," one of them said.

"My name is Connie, and this is Carol. What's your name, honey?"

"Richard," I said, "Are you enjoying yourselves?"

"Sure are," Carol said. "Where did you get that beautiful voice?"

"Born with it, I suppose," Connie answered for me.

"You could be a star," Carol added. "We know people with connections in New York. We could help you out."

"Why don't you come back to our hotel with us tonight?" Connie said.

I was only too happy to oblige, and one night turned into a wild, extended weekend. When they eventually left Parkersburg they gave me their address and phone number in New York City. "When you're ready, call us," they said. "You can live with us and we'll get you connected."

When I told Jim Angel I was leaving and going to New York, he took it in his good humored way.

"I knew you wouldn't last here," he said, tongue-in-cheek. "As soon as we made it to the big-time in Belpre, I knew you were gone. From Belpre you can only go to New York."

We promised to stay in touch. Unfortunately, after Belpre I lost track of Reuben Seegars. (I hope it's been a good life, Reuben, wherever you are).

In the spring of 1964, with my guitar, my suitcase, and a measly $87 in my pocket, along with Connie and Carol's phone number, I boarded a Greyhound bus for New York.

Turley, Jim Angel, and Ruben Seegers at
The Continental Club in Parkersburg, West Virginia (1964)

CHAPTER 7

Left West Virginia in the fall of '64,
A young man with a burning desire.
You see I'm a singer, and a good one I've been told,
And like thousands before me, I seek the pot of gold.
West Virginia Superstar,
Play and sing on your guitar.
Catch a dream and put it in a jar,
Oh West Virginia Superstar.[3] (Richards, 1974)

I was twenty-two when I arrived in New York City, an age when most people graduate college with their hard-earned degrees, leaving behind their protected lives and venturing out into the real world. I was pretty much the same; I just hadn't gone to college.

New York, both diverse and electric, made me see life differently. I thought I had pretty liberal attitudes toward race and justice, but I was still a southern country boy before I moved to New York. The city changed me for the better and made me grow out of my rural and limited attitudes. In a way, I grew up in New York.

I never imagined one place could offer so much variety. I was overwhelmed by the different nationalities, the selection of restaurants, and the polarization of the different neighborhood sections. It was like going to The World's Fair. Some of it was amazing, some of it was disturbing, but it would all take some getting used to.

When I arrived in New York, my two patrons, Connie and Carol were expecting me and, true to their word, let me move into a room in their penthouse apartment in Sutton Place. It was in one of the swankiest neighborhoods in Manhattan. I couldn't figure out how they could afford it because neither of them appeared to have a job. My guess was that they were somebody's "trophies," and they looked and played their parts with glamour and sex appeal. They were somebody's trophies then, but I soon found out that I was to be theirs. Not that I really minded, at least not at the start.

They may have been sincere about helping me, but in the meantime, Connie and Carol meant to enjoy their new toy, sharing me back and forth. I was happy to go along for the ride, especially since I figured their "connections" would no doubt soon come to fruition.

When we weren't having fun at Sutton Place, I would go out and explore my new home on the Upper East Side, looking out at the East River to Brooklyn and Queens. Nearly every weekend we would go to some big party or dinner, moving around in Connie and Carol's world of the wealthy, the powerful and, as it turned out, somewhat legally questionable.

---

[3] *West Virginia Superstar,* Turley Richards 1974, Almo Music, BMI.

"We have a big wedding to go to next weekend," said Connie "The daughter of one of our friends is getting married."

"Sounds cool," I said.

"Better still," Carol added. "You're going to sing at the reception."

Even if they didn't have so called "connections," Connie and Carol were definitely "connected." I didn't know it until we got there, but I had been engaged to sing at a true "family" wedding. Hollywood couldn't have cast it better, with what looked like half of Brooklyn, Queens, and New Jersey eating and dancing in a big hall. Wise guys, their wives and girlfriends, elderly relatives from the old country, and business associates spread all over. Presiding over the festivities was the uncle of the groom who must have been the Big Boss himself.

Connie introduced me, "This is Richard from West Virginia," she said.

The uncle turned to me with his big grin.

"Heyyy, how you doin', Richie? So you're the kid whooz gonna sing for us, huh? Connie says you sing great. All right, we'll let ya know when we're ready."

The reception rolled along, everyone applauded for the bride and groom, and I met a lot of people named Johnny and Jackie. When he was ready, the uncle, like Caesar at the Forum, lifted his hand for silence ... and ... it was as though the sound had gone out in a theatre! It was show time.

I thought to myself, "Holy crap, Richard, if you're ever going to do a great show, today's the day."

I got lucky because my audience was in a real party mood and wanted to hear rock 'n' roll. Some Chuck Berry, some R&B, a little scatting jazz, and I had won them over.

Since they seemed like the type of crowd that puts their all into both work and fun, I got everyone out of their seats and involved in sing-alongs.

"Okay," I announced. "Now let's sing 'Do you Wanna Dance'! Do you know it?"

A roar of approval.

"All right, this time I want you to join in at the end. First the women, and then the men." And I started singing, "Well, do you wanna dance and hold my hand. Tell me I'm your lover man ..."

I went through the first chorus: "Do you, do you, do you, do you wanna dance? Do you, do you, do you, do you wanna dance?"

Near the end I pointed to the women, who took over like a hundred Shirelles: "Do you, do you, do you, do you wanna dance? Do you, do you, do you, do you wanna dance?

"Great! Now the men!" I shouted. The Shirelles were gone, replaced by a hundred booming Al Capones: "Doo-yah, doo-yah, doo-yah, doo-yah wanna danzzz! Doo-yah, doo-yah, doo-yah, doo-yah, wanna danzzz!"

The women fell over themselves laughing. "Eh! What's a matta?" the men cried, throwing up their arms. It took all of my control to keep from laughing with the women.

"Okay," I said. "Ladies, I think you need to help the men out here."

"Whatta ya mean!" came their mock protests.

"All right," I said. "One more time! Go, ladies!"

"Do you, do you, do you, do you wanna dance?! Do you, do you, do you, do you wanna dance?!"

"Now the men!"

"Doo-yah, doo-yah, doo-yah, doo-yah wanna danzz! Doo-yah, doo-yah, doo-yah, doo-yah wanna danzzz! Ohhhh bayyy-beee, doo-yah wanna danzzz!" It turned into a fun time, and a fond memory where I got a standing ovation and a couple of hundred dollars in handshake tips.

It was a fun night, but it didn't lead anywhere. Several weeks had gone by and there were still no connections.

One night, some women at a party came up to me and said, "Now we understand what Carol and Connie were bragging about."

At that moment it hit me—there were no "connections." Carol and Connie were just using me. What young guy wouldn't have fun with that arrangement? But it wasn't why I came to New York. I was dedicated to music and serious about my career. I took the money I had collected from tips, and one day when the girls were out, I packed my stuff, wrote a short note of thanks, and left. I still didn't know anyone in New York, and there is no Fred or Janice to take me in. I was not going home like my sister Carolyn. It was make or break, and defeat was no option.

With the little money I still had, I checked into a cheap flea-bag hotel. It was rundown and dirty, with roaches everywhere. It soon became apparent that it was also a place for gay men to either live or hook-up and a place to be themselves away from family and embarrassment. This was still the early 1960s, but New York had its own underground culture where what was considered unacceptable by society could have its outlet. I saw a lot of crazy stuff in the community bathroom down the hall, got a few offers, but made a point of keeping my distance.

I needed to earn a living, but as in LA, I was adrift. It was the early summer of 1964 and the Beatles had swept through town that winter. The British invasion was on, but I was a musical snob—I thought that anything that wasn't R&B or Jazz just wasn't good music. Now everyone wanted to hear British pop, but I didn't like it. I hadn't been down to Greenwich Village much because it was the land of the folkies, with Bob Dylan the crowned king; but even Dylan was trying to move on by creating his own genre of "Folk-Rock."

The music scene was changing fast and I needed to find my foothold, but how and where? Nothing much was going on musically above the Village except in Harlem, but the sad reality was if you were white, you were told never to go north of 96th street unless you wanted trouble.

Soon I was out of money. I had to pay a week in advance at the fleabag, so I had paid the rent on Monday. By Friday, I hadn't eaten in five days. I had heard that a local blood bank was giving $25 for a pint of blood, but I was so weak when I went to the blood bank that I passed out on the table. They wisely refused to take from me what little strength I had left.

Leaving the building I twisted my ankle and stumbled to my knees on the edge of the curb. There in the gutter was about a $1.50. A measly windfall, but to a hungry man it was a pot of gold. I picked up the money and bought two Snickers bars and a couple of sodas. My options were limited, but I was going to enjoy this meal. I went back to my room at the flea bag and then made a dinner setting of a fork and knife with the Snickers bars sitting in the middle. Slowly, I cut into the candy bar and began eating it like it was a prime steak. When I was almost finished I took the last little piece, opened a drawer that was always filled with cockroaches, and threw it in. "Here guys," I said. "Enjoy your dinner."

I packed up my stuff because I didn't have enough money to stay another night, and headed for Central Park. I'm not sure why I went to the Park. I guess I thought I could find some comfort and privacy. It didn't hurt that it was free. For the next week or so Central Park would be my home. I was homeless. And a little bit scared.

Waking up after my first fitful night in the park, I accepted that the fix I was in was of my own making. If I had been lured by Connie and Carol's charm, then it was because I was naïve. I was determined to find a way out, but it was going to take some planning, so for the time being the Park would be my home. The possibility of giving up and going home to South Charleston had never crossed my mind. I knew sleeping in the open was risky, so I stayed close to the edge of the park, usually near Central Park West by the entrance to 72nd street, across from the old Dakota Hotel. I figured the more foot traffic, the safer I would be. The police would come through every so often and tell me to "move along," but I would wait until they left and then find another place to settle down. I probably looked too big to mess with, but I took precautions. While I slept, I left my belt on and hooked it through the handle of my guitar case. I used my suitcase as a pillow, so no one could move them without disturbing me. For drinking and washing up, I had to rely on the public water fountains. I was lucky—the weather was warm, and it didn't rain.

The first day in Central Park, I sat by a large pond and watched people come and go while I tried to create a plan. The second day I was exploring the surrounding neighborhoods when I noticed an outdoor café where a guy was singing to the lunchtime crowd. Every so often he would pass his hat around, asking for a tip for his efforts. The hat would work its way around and usually come back to him with a few dollars in it. "Passing the Hat" was something I'd seen before and vowed I'd never do. I was above that, but now I didn't have any room for false pride. I needed to survive. If that guy could do it and make a couple of bucks, then I could do it too because the guy stunk. If he was able to make some money, then I could do a lot better.

I began approaching some of the neighborhood cafes and pubs where I asked the owners if I could sing for my meals and be allowed to pass my hat. The first guy agreed, so I asked "can you lend me a hat?" The owner laughed and gave me a brandy snifter to pass around. Before long it would come back full. I was earning money, and although it wasn't enough to get a place to live, at least I had some cash in my pocket and I was no longer starving.

Every night I would return to the 72nd Street entrance. Away from the lights and traffic of Columbus Circle, the Park looked forbidding. Some nights I felt as though I were back in Don Hixson's car, parked on the Pennsylvania Turnpike and looking up at the stars. At dawn I awoke with the city, usually with a film of dew covering my clothes and guitar case. My focus stayed on getting a break, but when I wasn't playing for my lunch and dinner, I stayed in the park and kept to myself.

One day, an old man approached me and asked if he could share my bench near the pond. "Sure," I said, and we passed the time with small talk.

"By the way, what's your name?" he eventually asked.

"Richard," I said. "And yours?"

"Sam, here," he answered.

Then he asked me if I could spare some change. I didn't have much, but I gave him a dollar and he thanked me and walked away. Oh well, I thought, so much for my new friend. To my surprise, he came back a few minutes later with a big loaf of day-old bread and two sodas. For the next few days we met at the same place to talk. I found out he was from Buffalo, he was eighty-seven, his wife had died, and he had run away from home because his kids wanted to put him in a nursing home.

"No chance," he said, his blue eyes twinkling in the sunlight. "I've been independent my whole life, and I'm not going someplace where I'm supposed to just sit around and wait to die."

His story hit me hard. Was that the reward after a long life—to be forgotten and cast aside? Sam admitted that he was living in the Park, but he didn't say where and I thought it might be impolite to ask.

One day, I confided in Sam about Connie and Carol, and how they had lied to me.

"Can you really blame them?" Sam asked. "They were just being what they were. Besides, do you think they meant any harm?"

"No, probably not," I said.

"Lying is just a way of getting or believing in what you can't otherwise have, that's all," Sam added. "But it becomes a prison for the liar."

I told him that in my low moments I had told plenty of my own tall-tales and lies. I need to compensate for what I wasn't, but could have been if my own mind had led me to tell people that I had been like my brother Frank—that I had been an All-State basketball star in high school, I had played for West Virginia University, that if it wasn't for my eyes I could have turned pro, and that I had come to New York because of the promise of a recording contract

"And why'd you say those things?" Sam asked, as he watched two swans glide across the pond.

"They weren't meant to hurt anybody. I just knew I could have been all of those things if it wasn't for my eyes."

"Woulda, coulda, shoulda. How do you know it would have turned out that way if you hadn't got hurt? Maybe you would have been a different person. Maybe it was your eyes that made you try as hard as you did. None of that matters now. It's about what you do today with what you've got that matters."

"I just wish I didn't feel the need to say that stuff," I said.

Whether Sam had told me his own tall-tales was entirely possible, but after he listened to my confessions for awhile, he turned to me with his intelligent eyes and his white hair and beard shining like one of Mom's Old Testament prophets.

"Richard," he said, "can I give you some good advice from an old man?"

"You sure can," I answered.

Sam broke into a little smile. "Son, as long as you tell the truth, you never have to remember anything."

His comment hit me like a ton of bricks, and calmed my soul. I felt released, and we said goodnight—I headed back to 72nd Street, and Sam returned to his own secret retreat. The next day I went back at our usual place, but he didn't show. Soon I wouldn't have to live in the Park anymore. During the next few months, I would still go back to our spot by the pond but I never saw Sam again.

43

CHAPTER 8

Always tell the truth," was Sam's final counsel. It was a simple code I would come to live by: be honest, especially with yourself. Music was my passion, and was the reason I left South Charleston. I was in a tough spot and I needed to get out of the Park, but I knew I had to stay in New York if I was going to be successful. I just couldn't put enough money together to pay for my own place. I was singing at as many pubs as I could every day, which in the end also got me out of the Park at night.

Women seemed to be attracted to me, and I sometimes wondered if it was because I was a singer. When I was on breaks, I would walk around and talk to people, and women often asked me to join them. Many times, we would end up back at her place, where invariably the subject would come up that I didn't have a place to live (perhaps the fact that I was carrying a suitcase with my guitar tipped them off). Usually the lady extended an offer to stay longer, which I readily accepted. I did follow Sam's advice though, and remained honest to myself and to her. I was dedicated to making it in New York, and wasn't willing to jeopardize that by losing my focus because of romance.

"Look," I would say, "I have to stay focused on my music. I'll sleep wherever you want— on your floor, on your couch, or in your bed, but if you tell me you want something more then I'll have to move on. This is your place, so if that doesn't work for you then I totally understand."

They all had their own apartments and were either students or trying to make it as actors or artists. Some had trust funds or were being helped by their families who were willing to pay for their lifestyles, while others had jobs. I suspected one of the girls I stayed with paid her rent by working as an expensive call girl.

I met a lot of beautiful girls, but I was always true to my word. If I sensed they wanted something more than our casual arrangement, then I moved on. An invitation to visit her parents for the weekend told me it was time to leave so while she was at her job or class I would pack up my things and leave a short note expressing my gratitude and thanks for her help.

I wanted to get a day job, but I wasn't sure what I could do with my inability to see well. I did know I needed to earn enough money to get a place of my own. Ironically, a job contact came from Bonnie Boone, a girl I dated in LA. Bonnie was a model who had found work in New York, so when she was ready to come east she called my mom and got my number. We talked, and she told me she was coming to New York for a bikini modeling gig.

"You live in Southern California, and you're coming to New York to model bikinis?" I asked. We got a big laugh out of that one.

I helped Bonnie get settled into an apartment and we began seeing each other again. One night she took me to a party where I sang for the guests. Afterward I was introduced to Eddie Hershman who, with his brother, owned the Goya Guitar Factory in New York.

"You sure have a terrific voice," Hershman said. "Too bad I don't have any way of hiring you as a singer. But Bonnie says you need work and I always need strong guys like you down at the warehouse; would you be interested?"

I needed money and knew that I could easily handle the work, but I wasn't sure if my vision would be a problem.

"Mr. Herschman, my vision isn't too good, but I want the job and I'll give it a shot."

That Monday I went down to the Goya warehouse by the loading docks where boxes of electric guitars were loaded onto trucks for shipment. It was heavy work! One guitar may not weigh much, but a dozen together in a single crate calls for some muscle.

The work wasn't a problem, but what I hadn't realized was how dimly lit the warehouse would be, which created a pretty hazardous workplace for me. Before coming to New York I had gotten the contact lens for my right eye, which improved my sight but reduced my peripheral vision. It was like looking through a porthole, and the dim light made things worse.

I made some friends around the warehouse, one of which was a black guy named Cap who was a pretty tough guy whom no one messed with. We hit it off right away, talking about our shared love for R&B and Jazz.

One day when he wasn't around, the other guys told me why nobody ever messed with Cap. A few years earlier, five Italian hoods tried to collect "protection money" from him, which meant that if he paid them a monthly fee, they wouldn't beat him up. I was told that Cap told them to shove it up their asses and then proceeded to send all five of them to the hospital. That's why nobody messed with Cap. Good story, and it made me very happy that he was my friend.

I was moving some boxes on a hand truck one day when I came around a corner and accidently clipped a guy named Dominic. Dominic was a troublemaker who had a dangerous habit of inventing problems just to make trouble.

"Sorry man," I said as I went by.

"Fuck you!" Dominic yelled. "You did that on purpose!"

"What the hell are you talking about?"

"I think you did! Maybe I should fuck you up!"

"What the fuck?" I just kept going.

But Dominic wasn't done. The next day he came up with a hand truck and rammed it into a stack of crates I was standing on.

"Dominic," I said, "now, what the hell is that all about?"

"This is it!" he yelled, "I'm going to beat the fuck out of you!"

"C'mon," I answered as I jumped down, "let's get this over with."

With that he whipped out a Hawksbill knife—a knife tooled for cutting and slashing with a blade that curves down like a claw. Dominic crouched a little with the blade pointing up. If he got the chance, he meant to gut me.

"Why are you pulling a fucking knife on me?" I said. "You can't fight with your fists?"

"Because I'm gonna cut you up, pretty boy." Dominic crouched a little more, but then he suddenly straightened up when he saw somebody standing behind me. It was Cap.

"Put that goddamn knife away."

"This ain't any of your business, Cap." Dominic said.

"It's my business all right. Richard's my friend, and I don't like you."

Dominic looked terrified, probably because he was seeing himself lying broken in the street just like the five hoods a few years ago. He didn't want any part of Cap.

"Are you going to put that on me?" Cap said to him. "Put it away, or I'm gonna shove it up your ass."

Dominic did as he was told and folded the knife.

"Now," Cap said, "If something happens to my friend Richard after today, I'm gonna hold you responsible."

Cap's message was clear and Dominic stayed away from me. I only worked there a few more weeks, though; it just wasn't safe for me, even without nuts like Dominic.

"Thanks Cap," I said.

"No problem, Richard, you're the man."

I've always wondered why they called him "Cap."

I was without a job again, so I could no longer afford the boarding rooms where I had been living since I quit staying with girls. The job had allowed me to quit all that, but now it was gone. I hated being dependent on someone else to have a place to live, and I hated that I didn't have enough money to further my career. I also felt bad that needing a roof over my head had reduced me to using my body to get what I needed. I knew in my heart that without my lack of vision I would never have done it. Don't get me wrong, I was a virile young man, but this wasn't the way I wanted my life to be. The thought of ending up back in the Park with nothing to eat and no way to stay clean kept me doing what I needed to do.

I had enough money to stay at the boarding house a couple more nights, but didn't know where I was going to go after that. One of the guys at the boarding house told me that there was a strip on 41st Street between 7th and 7th Avenues that had a lot of opportunities for people to engage in "alternative" lifestyles. He told me that some of the guys at the boarding house would go down there and hang around on the street. After a while a limousine would pull up with a businessman in it. These men would pick up the guys on the street and take them for a ride, paying $50 to let the businessman perform oral sex on them or $100 to engage in more.

I went down there the next day and sure enough, after a few minutes a car pulled up in front of me. The back door opened and I got in. The car pulled away from the curb and almost immediately a male voice said, "You know it's $50, right?"

"Yeah, I know."

I felt his hand on my thigh and he said, "Baby you're really—"

"Stop the car, I can't do this!"

He started to try to talk me out of it, and I said, "Mister, you want to stop this car right now, and let me out."

The man signaled to his driver to pull over. I yanked the door open and got out. I remember going to the nearest doorway, where I stood like a statue with tears running down my face. All I could think was, "My God, is this what my life has come to?" Then I just started walking.

On my way back to the boarding house, my luck changed when I noticed a sign on the window of the New York Art Academy asking for models. The pay was $25 an hour. I went inside and asked the woman at the desk about the sign. She gave me a once over and said, "You'll do fine. Oh, and by the way, you do know that it's in the nude."

"It's in the what?" I asked.

"You model for the students in the nude while they sketch you. Will that be a problem?"

"Well, no. For $25 I'll do almost anything." She had no idea where I had just come from.

"Good," she said, and she told me where to go.

It was definitely a strange and different experience at first, but it got a little better with time. The only problem was that the classes and opportunities to model were few and far between. I desperately needed money.

One day after a session, I hooked up with one of the art students, an attractive girl named Gwynne who promised that she wasn't looking for a serious relationship. That became apparent a few nights later, when she began inviting her girlfriend Rita over to join us.

One night Rita said to me, "I hear you're tight for money. Have you ever thought of making movies?

"Movies? What kind of movies?"

"Just doing what we're doing here. You know, sex movies. You'll make a lot of money."

"How much money?" I asked.

I found out it would be $500 per movie. The first thing I saw in my head was me in my own apartment, with a chance to work on my career. Compared to what I almost did on 41st Street a few days earlier (and for far less money), this seemed like a piece of cake. If making a movie like this was going to give me back my independence and my freedom, then I was damn well going to do it.

I went down to the "film studio," which turned out to be another warehouse like the one I had worked in for Goya Guitars. The producer/director turned out to be a little chunky gay guy who wanted his new leading man naked during the interview. He struck a pose with his hands on his hips, and lisped, "You know, we're used to guys with ten or more."

I wasn't fazed. "Well, I'm six feet four, so if I were a little guy like you it'd look like a tree trunk."

The director giggled and replied, "It would, it would indeed."

"But I do have some conditions," I said.

"Oh, like what?"

"I don't want anybody to see who I am. I need to wear a mask."

The director thought fast, and a "plot" was quickly spun that would allow me to conceal my face. The required props were found, and we were ready to shoot.

It's almost too sad and embarrassing to talk about now, but I was cast to be the leading stud of two "westerns," one titled *Who's That Masked Man?* and the other *The Bone Ranger Rides Again.* The second title basically summed up both plots. In my defense, I wasn't completely naked—the Bone Ranger wore his mask, boots, a cowboy hat, and toy cap guns with holsters. One of my big lines was, "Baby, this here's a six shooter." When the director yelled, *"Cut!"* Gwynne and Rita, who were my co-stars, had to be told to "break it up." This was definitely not high-class cinema.

I never found out what became of the movies, nor did I really care. I was just thankful they never surfaced where anyone I knew could see them, and to this day I pray to God that Mom never knew. What was important was that I made $1,000, and that kept me from being homeless again. I had done a lot just to survive over the past few months. All I needed now was to be seen and heard by the right people.

I had saved enough money to get a place of my own, and rented a basement apartment on Charles Street in Greenwich Village. It was windowless and long and dark like a cave, with a portable refrigerator and an old stone sink, but for at least the month's rent I had paid, it was home. I needed something to happen, though, or I would be back on the street.

"Always tell the truth," Sam said. Before I moved into Charles Street I had stayed with a total of thirteen women. One night I was playing in a pub when the last woman I stayed with, an aspiring actress named Helen, came in. As it turned out, Helen was my lucky thirteen. When I finished singing she came up to me. I didn't know what to expect and thought that maybe she wanted trouble.

"You know," she said, "I was pretty hurt when you just up and left. I felt used, until I remembered that you were honest with me from the beginning. You told me that you were committed to your music career and you didn't want a relationship. You didn't lie or try to trick me, and because you were honest with me I want to help you." Helen handed me a piece of paper with a name and phone number written on it. "Call him," she said. "He's a big time manager and he'll get you started."

I looked at the name Helen had written on the paper: "Norman Schwartz."

CHAPTER 9

Toward the end of 1964, the Village music scene was hot, and not just with folk music, but with R&B, Jazz, and rock 'n' Roll, played out nightly in legendary clubs like the Blue Note, the Village Gate, Gerde's Folk City, the Café Wha?, the Half Note, and the Bitter End. Like the thousands of artists who still make Greenwich Village their home, I worked hard as I tried to further my career. During the day I would head over to Washington Square Park and set myself up in a corner apart from the painters, poets, beatniks, and the other musicians. Eventually I would attract a crowd, playing for the tips some tossed into my guitar case, or sometimes passing the hat. At night I played at the clubs.

Since we were mostly eager unknowns looking for a break and an audience, the pay wasn't much, maybe $25 to $30 a night, but it was better than passing the hat. I played regularly at the Café Wha? on McDougal Street. The Wha? Was started in the '50s by Manny Roth, and became one of the spots in the Village where new talent would bring their dreams. For six or seven weeks I was in the regular lineup with three future stars of music, movies, and television. One was a folk singer from Brooklyn named Richie Havens. Richie always opened since he had another engagement across town. The Wha? was also a place for young comics, and in between Richie and me, a yet unknown, David Frye, would come out and do his dead-on impersonations of politicians and celebrities. David would then introduce me.

The Wha? was in a narrow basement room with the door to the stairs in one corner and a small stage or performing area halfway down the room on the left. Because the stage was so small, I'd stand with my guitar, and dance in place while playing Jackie Wilson, the Isley Brothers, and Chuck Jackson. Playing with me with his standup bass was Bill Takas, who would eventually join Doc Severinsen's *Tonight Show* band. Bill and I usually finished with the Isley Brother's "Shout," which is the kind of song that brings down the house. It also wasn't easy for another singer to follow, so the Wha? put a second young comedian after me.

"Thank you everyone," I would say. "Now please welcome Richard Pryor!" Pryor would come out and do what would later become his famous routine about the problems of being both black and Italian living in a Jewish tenement in a Puerto Rican neighborhood.

One night after I had finished with "Shout" and left the Wha? shaking and rocking, Pryor came out to start his routine. Dressed in a dark suit, he cupped his right elbow into his left hand. Waving the mike in front of his mouth like a metronome he then went into a purposefully out-of-tune version of "Shout." "Shooouuuut, woooo, Shooouut, wooooo. Dammmmnnn!" he said, "Richard ain't nothing but a nigger trapped in a white man's body!" The audience broke down laughing, and I couldn't resist joining in with a Step 'n' Fetchit impersonation.

"I is, boss!" I yelled, "I *is*! I'se gonna shine your shoes, press yo' pants, I'se here for ya, boss! Anything you want, I is—" Pryor broke up.

"I is, boss!"

Pryor was doubled over laughing so hard he could hardly catch his breath. "C'mon Richard," he finally said, "let me do my act."

"Alright boss, but I *is!*" The audience ate it up.

Afterward in what passed as the Wha's? dressing room, Pryor sidled up to me and punched me in the arm. "Man, I just knew you weren't prejudiced," he said.

"No man, I'm not prejudiced! I own three of you down in West Virginia." Pryor broke up again as he had on stage. It was probably the only answer that could have won him over, and he responded with his not-yet-famous line.

"You know, if you weren't such a big son-of-a-bitch, I'd kick your ass." He had been standoffish until that night, but our little improvisation had broken the ice, and we became friends. We would share forty more shows together at the Wha? Often at the end of the night we would go out for breakfast, jiving and talking.

As it turned out, we had some things in common. We were the same age, and with unconventional childhoods, neither of us had finished high school. We both had come to New York to "make it," and were still working toward our big break. Superstardom awaited Pryor, but in these early days he was just a fun guy to be around and we could make each other laugh. I sensed there was some pain behind the offstage shyness, and doing stand-up must have been his way of overcoming it.

We got to know each other a little better on the nights we went out to breakfast, and one night Pryor shared with me that he grew up in a brothel in Peoria where his grandmother was the Madam, and his mother was one of the house girls. Pryor told me that his most painful memory from childhood was lying in bed at night trying to fall asleep while he could hear his mother down the hall servicing a john.

When Richard shared his story with me of his personal pain, I was touched by his honesty and rawness and I found myself sharing with him my nightmare of being raped over a period of three years beginning at age eleven.

When I finished the story, Richard was sympathetic, but couldn't help himself, saying, "Damn! Even though that happened, that was still kinda cool, wasn't it?" Typical male response!

The Half Note was famous for having all-star jazz players jamming on Monday nights, so if I wasn't performing, I would go there to listen.

I was sitting at the bar basking in the reflected glory of eleven incredible jazz musicians, when the bartender said to me, "they want you to come up and sing."

"Do what?" I said. The bartender repeated himself, and all I could say was, "I have all of their albums!"

Now, I never get nervous about singing, but this time I was a little intimidated. The decision was taken out of my hands, when someone on stage said into the mic, "Hey, we got a young singer who's gonna come up and join us. C'mon, man."

I don't want to bore you, but lovers of jazz will understand. On the stage that night were: drums, Max Roach; bass, Ray Brown; piano, Hank Jones; guitars, Jimmy Hall and Tao Farlow; saxophones, Gerry Mulligan, Stan Getz, and Sonny Stith; trumpets, Kenny Durham and Freddie Hubbard, and on valve trombone, Erbie Green.

I sang a Count Basie/Joe Williams song titled *Well, Oh Well* and I scatted my ass off! When the song was over, the band applauded me. It was the thrill of my life.

After the show I got another thrill. "Hey kid," someone said. I turned around to find Max Roach standing behind me.

"Yes Mr. Roach," I said.

"I'm sure you've heard that I don't like white people," he said.

"Yes sir, I've heard that."

"But I've got to tell you something," Roach went on. "You're one hell of a motherfuck'n scat phenom." Before I had a chance to reply, he turned and walked away.

I was in jazz heaven. The next day I called Jim Angel back in Charleston and told him about the night.

"Can you believe it, Jim? I shared a stage with these guys and Max Roach said I was a motherfuck'n scat phenom!"

"Shit, Richard," Jim said, "you've made it. You might as well come home now."

Helen had given me Norman Schwartz's name during a weekend gig, so I called his office on Monday. He took my call, and I told him that Helen had given me his number. He asked me to come in the next Thursday and to be sure to bring my guitar.

Norman Schwartz was a show business manager with a list of artists that included the saxophonist Stan Getz, the composer and arranger Gary McFarland, and singers like Mel Torme and Morgana King. Schwartz was around forty, with an honest reputation and a heart and smile as big as the city he grew up in. If you were one of his clients, then you were part of his family, with weekends at his beach house on Fire Island or afternoons at Yankee Stadium, where sitting one day listening to the action on a transistor radio I watched my hero Mickey Mantle bat and take the field.

With Norman Schwartz running my career, I was in for a real lifestyle change and wouldn't need to think of ways to simply survive anymore. First, he moved me out of Charles Street and into the landmark Chelsea Hotel. The Chelsea, a red brick building that resembled an overgrown schoolhouse, was famous for its resident musicians, artists, and bohemians of all kinds. I had windows, and there weren't any cockroaches, but there were plenty of characters. One afternoon in the elevator, a beautiful bohemian girl invited me up to her penthouse for tea. I thought I was going to have a romantic encounter, but while we were sitting having tea in her living room I encountered no less than a six-foot boa constrictor, a big, hairy tarantula, and a scorpion. They were all pets. I am not kidding, I would not make this stuff up! I couldn't get out of there fast enough.

Norman Schwartz was the best manager I would ever have. "He really cared about you Turley," his widow would tell me many years later. "He thought you had the best voice he'd ever heard. He just loved you." Schwartz had a record deal for me in no time with MGM/Verve, but before I made a new record I had a new name, courtesy of Norman Schwartz.

I was in Norman's office one day when Stan Getz walked in. "Come here Stan, I want you to meet my new artist, Turley Richard."

Getz recognized me. "Wait, man," he said, "aren't you the young kid who sat in with us down at the Half Note? Man, Norman, this son-of-a-bitch can sing!"

While Stan told him that I had wowed all the jazz players over at the Half Note, I went over to a desk and began writing my name the way Schwartz had said. Turley Richard. I kind of liked it. When playing basketball back home, everyone had always referred to me as "Turley," and I had even toyed with dropping my first name and becoming simply "Turley" as a stage name. But I liked Turley Richard.

When Stan left, Schwartz came over and I pushed the piece of paper over to him. "Hey Norman, what do you think of this?"

Schwartz looked at me with an apologetic look on his face. "I'm sorry, I have a form of dyslexia where I turn names around."

"Oh it's okay, man, I really like it, but there's something missing."

Schwartz bent over the desk, looked at the paper for a moment, and then said, "Oh, here we go." He wrote an "s" at the end of Richard. It worked, and I became Turley Richards.

I recorded a single for MGM, *Since You've Been Gone/What's Your Name* with Jerry Ragavoy and Creed Taylor producing. Taylor was already an established name in the jazz world, having recruited John Coltrane for his previous label, and Ragavoy would someday write for Janis Joplin and produce Bonnie Raitt. We used a recording studio in New York and MGM loved it, but they never promoted it so nothing happened. It was like DOT records all over again, but this time I had a manager, and wouldn't be snubbed in a corporate headquarters lobby as I had been in Los Angeles. Schwartz quickly got me a new deal, this time with 20th Century Fox Records.

Twentieth Century wanted to get into the "blue-eyed soul" market, and thought that I would be their star. Gary McFarland produced the album and he brought in some of the best jazz musicians in New York. One was Toots Theilemans, the great guitarist and harmonica player who at the time had a guest role on the country flavored *Jimmy Dean Show*. Theilemans would come to the recording session still dressed in his hayseed character's outfit from the show.

"Who's that little old guy in the overalls and what's he doing here?" I asked McFarland.

"Forget what he looks like," McFarland assured me. "When he starts to play, just watch the smoke rising from above the baffles."

He was right—Toots was great! So was Bill Takas, who joined me from the Wha? "The Many Souls of Turley Richards" was unique in that it was recorded in front of a live audience. I liked that, and I liked the musicians, but the album had many problems. We had a collection of jazz musicians trying to play R&B. Also, I could hit high notes and they were fast becoming my trademark, but were overused on the record. It just didn't work, and nothing sounded right to me. I felt sad about the whole thing, and I put a lot of the blame on Gary McFarland.

"He did a terrible job," I complained to Norman Schwartz.

"No he didn't," Schwartz replied, irritated with me. "You've got an album deal, so what's the problem?"

I did have an album deal, but I also wanted to make a good record, and I just couldn't hide my disappointment. Even the title didn't make any sense to me. Maybe Schwartz was right, and I needed to show a little gratitude. It was easy to forget that just the year before I had been homeless, sleeping in Central Park. Now here I was recording an album for a major record label. But I was still unhappy.

Things came to a head one weekend on Fire Island when Schwartz and I got into another argument about the album. Schwartz didn't like what I was saying, and thought I was giving him a bad attitude. Gary McFarland was not just his client, but also a friend and he felt he needed to stick up for him.

"The album isn't that bad," Schwartz insisted, "I don't know what you're talking about."

"Go back and listen to it, Norman," I said. "It isn't R&B, it isn't jazz—it isn't anything."

I found out years later that when others disagreed with him, Schwartz would dig in his heels and could out-stubborn anyone. I was stubborn too, but he was my manager, and looking back on it maybe he was right. I needed to show a little more gratitude and get over myself, but from my point of view the album totally missed the mark. We didn't speak after that for two months. If I had known about his stubborn side, maybe I would have apologized, but I was young and confident and had my own strong opinions about the music I should be playing. When my contract expired near the end of 1965, we parted ways. It really was a shame.

~ ~ ~ ~

I spent a few months on my own again before another opportunity came up. During this time, I hung around the gym during the days and continued playing the local clubs at night. While living at the Chelsea, I often worked out and played basketball at McBurny's YMCA across the street. One day after a workout, I was in McBurney's shower washing up. My peripheral sight wasn't good, but I could still see this little guy staring at me. I finished my shower and went into the locker room to get dressed, and there right behind me getting dressed was the guy from the shower. I finished dressing and went to the elevator, and there was the same guy slipping in before the door closed. I walked out onto 23rd Street, and right behind me was the same little guy. Finally I turned around and said, "What the hell do you want?"

The guy smiled. "Oh, nothing," he said, "but you have the most gorgeous buns I've ever seen."

I had never been spoken to that way by a man, and I was truly taken aback. I really didn't know how to respond, and it made me really nervous. I just wanted to get rid of the guy, so I used what I knew. I balled up my fists like I was going to hit him and took a step forward saying, "Why, you little—" but the guy didn't move! Hell, he didn't even blink! He just stood there smiling that weird little smile. I didn't know what to do next, so I just grumbled, "Screw off!" and then spun around and walked out into 23rd Street without looking. A horn blared and brakes screeched all around me as I crossed to the Chelsea.

Back in my room, it occurred to me what had really pissed me off. It was as though I was just a piece of fresh meat to this guy, and then I thought, "Is that what we make women feel like when we give them the once over look, a catcall, or whistle? Man," I thought, "are we pigs or what?" I decided right then that I would treat women differently in the future, and show them more respect. (However, I did check out my buns in the mirror!)

A few days later I was playing some one-on-one basketball at McBurney's. Defending against the guy I was playing, I put my hand on the small of his back while he tried to back up and take a shot at the hoop. That's where the game suddenly ended.

"You can't touch me!" the guy said.

"What are you talking about?"

"You can't put your hands on me. I'm not playing with you because you can't touch me."

He walked off the court in a huff. I just stood there, not really knowing what to think. We were only playing basketball, right? Then another guy who had witnessed the whole thing walked up to me and said with an overdone lisp, "Sssay, would you like to play some one-on-one?" Often we make friends where and when we least expect it.

What the hell? "Is everybody in New York queer?" I asked to no one in particular. The other guys around the gym broke up laughing. I'd been had. "Hi, my name's Mickey," he said, extending his hand.

"Hey, Mickey, my name's Turley. You got me. But really, is everybody in New York queer?"

Mickey Clark was a singer/songwriter from Louisville, Kentucky. A graduate from Purdue University, he came to New York the year before I did with his folk group, The Three of Us. "Why don't you come down and hear us sing?" Mickey asked me

"Sure, where?"

"The Night Owl Café over on 3rd Street."

Eventually I took Mickey up on his invitation and went to the Night Owl, and really enjoyed their music. The Three of Us broke up a little while later so Mickey started playing solo in a club on Bleecker Street called the Back Fence.

"You should come down there, Turley, it's a casual place. We don't get paid much but we have a good time just pick'n and grin'n."

The Back Fence, like the Wha?, was another narrow shotgun room with a bar, but on street level rather than in the basement. The Back Fence was quiet and informal. Originally a beat poet hangout, it supposedly got its name from Allen Ginsberg, one of the primary leaders of the Beat Generation. Now with beer barrels to sit on and peanut shells strewn across the floor, it was home to folkies.

When I went down there one afternoon it was just as Mickey said—everyone was sitting around talking and listening. After awhile, Mickey handed me a guitar, so I played and sang. The Fence's owner, Rocky Cinta, came over to talk. Rocky was the classic New York tavern keeper, a kind of informal businessman who would introduce himself as if he were already an old friend.

"Hey Richie," he said, "you want to play on the list?"

"Sure, but my name is Turley."

I figured I would get right down to business.

"Rocky, I would love to play here, but I don't want to sit on a barrel. I'd like to have a more show-biz atmosphere—maybe a stage and sound system over in that corner.

"You wanna do what?" Rocky asked.

'Yeah, I answered. "I'll pull them in. You want a crowd or not?"

"Yeah, but—"

Rocky and his family were notoriously tight-fisted. It was said that when the Back Fence had a kitchen fire and everyone ran for their lives, Rocky's mother ran after them yelling "Stop them, everyone's leaving without paying!"

Rocky thought it over for a minute. "Okay. Somehow I believe you."

"Listen, try it for four weeks. Put in an opening act, and then I'll play a couple of one-hour sets, and we'll pack the place."

That's how the Back Fence began its new life as a hot music spot. By my fourth weekend, the club was packed with lines out the door. Record labels started coming around to find out what the buzz was all about. Like the Back Fence, my career was taking a turn for the better, for it was from the Fence that word got back to Scandore and Shayne about this hot singer named Turley Richards that they just had to sign. Joe Scandore was an old-time promoter whose big acts included the comedians Don Rickles and Jonathan Winters. Together, Scandore and Mel Shayne managed the great Wilson Pickett and acts like the Kingsmen of *Louie Louie* fame. I was asked to come up to their office for an audition, which ironically was two floors below Norman Schwartz. I sang for Joe Scandore, Mel Shayne, their big band manager, Hermie Drexler, and producer and publisher Paul Tannen. When I started singing I could feel the energy in the room go up.

"Man," Drexler said to me, "You oughta be singing Jazz."

"Noooo," Mel Shayne said, "we want to make money."

Society was a lot less politically correct back then, so as soon as Mel Shayne started talking about money, Joe Scandore just couldn't help ribbing his partner.

"Just listen to the Jew," Scandore said.

"But I'm Jewish, too," Drexler protested.

"Yeah, but you love music,"

The camaraderie between them put me at ease, and I felt like I had come to the right place.

Things went well immediately with Scandore and Shayne who landed a deal with CBS/Columbia Records. Columbia records had Bob Dylan, Johnny Mathis, and many other great artists. Best of all, they wanted me to do real R&B.

In the beginning of 1966 I had new management, a new record deal, and another new address. From the Chelsea Hotel I moved to an apartment on Carmine Street, where I now had a kitchen and a living room that I filled with used furniture. Just a few blocks away were the Wha? and the Back Fence. I often crossed paths near the square with a guitarist who was new to the Village, Jimi Hendrix. Jimi had finished playing backup for the Isley Brothers and had just emigrated down from Harlem with his new band, the Blue Flame. Some afternoons I would pass Jimi on the street going the other way, barefoot and in jeans with a vest but no shirt. In a city of characters, Jimi still stood out. We got to be familiar to each other, and Jimi would smile and say "Hey chief" each time he saw me. Most days he looked like he was in another world, and could just as easily have been gliding instead of walking across 6th Avenue. He usually had a pencil stuck behind his ear while in his right hand he carried a handful of white napkins to write on.

I knew that Jimi had heard me sing, so one day I stopped him.

"Hey Jimi."

"Heeyyy Chief."

"Do you remember who I am?"

Jimi tried to focus on me, and then broke into a broad grin. "Yeah, man," he said. "You're that cat who can sing notes all the way up to Mars."

"Yeah," I said, "and you were there."

Jimi threw his head back, and laughed his stoner laugh, "Yeaahhh, I guess I was," he said, and then continued on his way to stardom.

My own path to stardom took me to Columbia Records. Scandore and Shayne had secured a deal for four sides, and they wanted me to do R&B and blue-eyed soul. I recorded my own songs, one of them being the soulful *I'm a Lonely Man*. My producer, Paul Tannen, booked some of the best black R&B musicians in New York for the sessions—the great drummer Bernard Purdie, bassist Chuck Rainey, and guitarists Eric Gale and Cornell Dupree. Even though we were working on the same record for the same label, the group Paul assembled seemed a little standoffish. It probably didn't help matters when I showed up at the studio in a muscle shirt, cutoff shorts, and sandals. I did apologize for the way I was dressed and told them I had just come from the beach.

Once we started playing I could feel that their attitude toward me was changing. Finally, after one hot take Bernard Purdie left his drum set, and crossed the room to hug me, "My god, brother, you sound like you must've sung in black churches!" I had won them over, and we made a hit record together.

Soon after *I'm a Lonely Man* was released, it started getting a lot of air play, and was soon in the top ten of all of the black stations across the country. One day I stopped by my producer's office. I opened Tannen's door but he wasn't alone.

"I'm sorry, Paul, I didn't know you were with anyone."

"C'mon in Turls," Paul said. The guy he was with turned around and I recognized Granny White, who was Columbia's head of promotions for Soul and R&B. White was short and stout and always reminded me of Fats Domino. He greeted me with a handshake and his big smile.

"Hey Turley," Granny said. "How are you?" Just as Granny said my name, I realized there was a third guy in Tannen's office.

"Turley Richards?" a voice from behind me asked. I turned around to find an elegantly dressed black man in a three-piece suit.

"Yeah," I answered.

"Turley Richards, as in *I'm a Lonely Man* Turley Richards?" The guy looked shocked.

"That's right."

"Damn! You're white!"

"And damn," I smiled, "you're black!"

"Turley," Granny broke in, "This is Wilson Pickett."

Now it was my turn to be shocked. "Man," I said to Pickett, "you're one of the best Soul singers alive!"

But Pickett wasn't listening. "God damn! You're white!" He hugged me; it was my initiation into the royalty of Soul and R&B.

Columbia was getting excited about *I'm a Lonely Man* and felt they had a real hit on their hands. All the record needed was a little promotion for it to climb up the charts. Promotion was something I'd never had before. I finally had a record company on my side.

To promote the record, Columbia put my picture in big ads for *I'm a Lonely Man* in *Cashbox* and *Billboard* magazines. A great first step, and when the black stations who had been giving me such a big push saw my face, they had the same reaction as Wilson Pickett—damn, Turley Richards is white! Overnight, they stopped playing *I'm a Lonely Man,* and without any air play that's just how *I'm a Lonely Man* died; unwanted and alone. I finally got some promotion, and it killed me. Go figure.

After *I'm a Lonely Man,* Columbia got cold feet about letting me do more R&B.

"Why not?" I asked. "If we keep making good records, then they can't be ignored."

But Columbia wanted me to go in a more pop R&B direction, and since I was still trying to establish myself, I felt I had to listen.

In order to attract more promotion, Scandore and Shayne arranged for me to audition with the William Morris Agency. William Morris was the biggest booking agency in the world, and I was pleasantly shocked that I was to audition for them. When I arrived at their offices I was ushered into an audition room, complete with piano and drums where I was expected to perform for nineteen executives. With me were a piano player and Bill Takas to play his upright base. I was singing, but not playing guitar for this one. There were nineteen men in the room, but no women. Like Elvis, my whole act was to sing and dance using a sensual appeal, and I felt really awkward doing this to a room full of men.

"Aren't you going to call in the secretarial pool for an audience?" I asked.

"Nahh, kid," said the head of the group with an unlit cigar clenched between his teeth. "Just play and show us what ya' got."

I turned to Bill Takas and whispered, "What the hell am I gonna do with no women here?"

"Just pretend your blind," Bill said, "and picture them all as women."

Years later, I would kid around with Bill and tell him that my blindness was all his fault.

It was a good idea—good enough to get a standing ovation from my all-male jury.

"That was great kid!" the leader said over his cigar. "How does a kid as big as you dance and move like that?"

Through William Morris I was (among other bookings) signed to be part of the Gene Pitney *Shower of Stars* tour in the latter half of 1966. Pitney was one of the few American pop stars from the early 1960s to have survived the British Invasion. Since he worked with the Rolling Stones, his popularity spanned both sides of the Atlantic. In the mid-60s Pitney put together a travelling music show featuring acts like BJ Thomas, Bobby Goldsboro, Norma Tanega, the McCoys, and Chad and Jeremy. Their music was definitely not my style, but again I needed promotion.

The tour took us through nearly the entire East, South, and Mid-West, with two stops across the border in Canada. Without a current record, I was an add-on, and while the other artists like Chad and Jeremy had their names in lights, I was relegated to the "and others" end of the billing.

We travelled almost exclusively by bus, from Buffalo and Montreal to Virginia Beach, Mobile, Tulsa, Little Rock, Rock Island, and Detroit. We did fly once from Kennedy Airport to Nashville, but by the end of that flight, we all wished we were back on the bus.

"Ladies and gentlemen, this is your pilot," the voice over the intercom said. "We're presently over London and experiencing some difficulty with our tail wing and will need to turn around and make an emergency landing."

"We're over London? How the hell did we get there?" that eased the tension a little as we all laughed and explained that we were over London, Kentucky, not London, England.

The tail wing was actually coming off the plane, and as we descended things got a little scary. I could just see the headlines: GENE PITNEY, "AND OTHERS" DIE IN PLANE CRASH.

As the plane spun its way down, I stood up and shouted, "I hope my mom knows who 'and Others' is when she reads about this!" Even though we were pretty scared, everyone laughed. We finally landed, but the plane spun around four times on the runway. Eventually, it was over and everyone "and others" were safe.

The bus rides were long, and we must have logged at least several thousand miles during the eight weeks of the tour. To pass the time, Gene Pitney would preside over poker games in the back of the bus. Not everyone was interested in playing, and soon boredom set in, which caused people to get short-tempered. One was a trumpet player who was hired to be part of the backup show band. He was an ex-Navy guy who had played trumpet in the Navy Band. One day on the bus he was riding the McCoys about their Beatles-style long hair and wouldn't let up.

"You know," he finally said to them, "someone could come up behind you and think you were a bunch of girls." The McCoys were just a group of teenage kids, and while they just sat and took it, I didn't think it was right.

"Hey, man," I said. "Why don't you just shut the fuck up? They're good kids, so leave them the hell alone."

"You shut the fuck the up," the guy said to me. "Tell me what to do again and I'm gonna beat the shit out of you."

"Hey, Bill, pull the bus over," I said

Bill replied, "With pleasure!" Nobody liked the guy.

I heard Gene Pitney cup his hands and yell up to me, "Turley, just don't hit him in the mouth!" Laughter from the bus followed me as we stepped off.

A few minutes later, they carried him back on the bus and we were on our way. The McCoy's hair was never an issue again.

The crowds we drew were enthusiastic and I was performing my style of music, but they were mostly teens looking for bubble-gum. Since I wasn't promoting a record, I was only allotted two songs, so I chose two that showed off my dance ability—Jackie Wilson's *Lonely Tear Drops* and James Brown's *I Feel Good*. Although I didn't quite fit with the pop sounds of the McCoys or Chad & Jeremy, the audience still loved it.

The tour finally wrapped up in Detroit, and although I wanted to get back to New York and my scheduled recording sessions, it had been a fun time with a lot of good memories. It's common for performers on the road to play pranks on each other at the end of the last show on the tour, and we wanted to go out with a laugh, so the McCoys and I planned a little prank for Gene Pitney. Little did we know that Pitney would set himself up for his own funny send-off. Gene couldn't have been a nicer and more unassuming guy, but he still liked to play the star during shows.

The last show of the tour, we were playing the Ford Theatre, which had a stage with an orchestra pit that could be mechanically raised level with the stage. Pitney thought this would be a great way to make his entrance, so he planned to come through the door onto the orchestra pit that would raise him up to the stage.

Unfortunately, they didn't rehearse the idea.

When it came time for Gene to make his entrance, the emcee said, "Now welcome the star of our show, *Gene Pitney!*" The band began its intro, but no Gene Pitney. We heard a loud banging on the door, which was stuck and wouldn't open. The muffled banging went on for about a minute with the band playing the same four bars of intro music over and over. One of the crew was headed over to help, when Gene finally kicked it open.

Slowly the platform rose with Gene singing one of his hits, and as soon as he became visible to the audience, they went wild. He was getting into his song, when the platform started down again and Pitney slowly disappeared. The platform rose again, but this time it stopped halfway up before it again began its descent. Gene kept singing, but he was looking pretty freaked out, and was sweating buckets from his fight with the door. With each trip up and down everyone saw a little less Pitney. On the last trip up, only his head was visible.

As he began his inevitable descent to the bottom of the orchestra pit, I decided I better help him, so I ran out on stage, yelling "Gene!" and motioning him to come over to me. I dropped to my knees and hauled him by his armpits onto the stage. Gene yelled his thanks to me as I ran off.

Pitney was about to do his last song, and was thanking the audience for coming out, when I walked on stage in only my tightey-whities and a towel over my shoulder. "Hey Gene," I called, in by best Gomer Pyle voice, "You know where they keep the soap?"

Gene Pitney turned back to the audience. "Well, that's Turley Richards, the funniest guy we've ever had on tour with us, but if you meet only one Turley in your life, it's enough."

CHAPTER 10

New York City at three in the morning can be eerily empty and quiet, like a city of ghosts. I found my way to Carmine Street and walked up to my apartment door. Home for the first time in months, I tried my key. It wouldn't fit the lock. Maybe I was holding it at the wrong angle? I tried the lock again. Did I have the wrong key? I didn't have that many keys. Was I in the right building, at the right door? After riding around in a bus all summer I suddenly wondered if I was in the right city? I tried again. What the—

I went outside. Father Demo Park was lit but empty, and except for the occasional taxicab rocketing past, so was Sixth Avenue. Now what? I thought of my friend Bill Takas who had an apartment just a few blocks away.

"What happened, Turley?" Bill said when I woke him up.

"I don't know, but my key wouldn't work."

"Was there a sign on the door?"

"I think there was, but I couldn't read it. The letters were too small."

"C'mon, let's see what it said."

We walked back to Carmine Street and up to my apartment door.

"Ummm, Turley," Bill said after reading the sign. "You've been evicted."

"I've been what!"

A little lesson in city living: decent apartments are prized possessions that you don't let go of easily, especially in New York. I had sub-let my apartment on Carmine from a guy named Neil. Neil was the actual renter who didn't want to give up the apartment, even though he wasn't living there. So to keep the lease (and make a little profit) Neil rented his apartment to me. I gave my rent money to Neil, and then Neil paid his rent to the landlord. It was a neat deal where I got a place to live, Neil kept the lease, the landlord got his money, and everyone was happy. But there were two problems: first of all, sub-letting was illegal, and second, Neil turned out to be a crook who was taking my money but neglecting to pay the rent. So, when I was walking onstage in my tighty-whities, the landlord cancelled Neil's lease, took all of my furniture and the clothes I had left behind while on tour, and auctioned it all off.

Since sub-letting was illegal I had no rights or legal recourse. Fortunately I managed to track down the guy who bought some of my things, including the tailored suits I bought when I was with Norman Schwartz.

"I'm a singer trying to make it, and I got screwed by the guy who should have been paying the rent," I explained. "That's my stuff, so let me give you what you paid for it."

The guy was a shifty hard ass. "You got a receipt? Can you prove this stuff belonged to you?"

My name was on the monthly bill for the television set, but other than that I didn't have any real proof, but who would bother making up a story like that, and the guy knew it.

"Look," I said, "the suits are obviously mine. How many six-foot four-inch 220-pound guys are walking around with tailored suits? I'll give you $400 for them."

"Well you still can't prove they're yours, so give me a $1,000 and the suits are yours." As soon as he said this, the guy was sorry, because Richard Turley, not Turley Richards, was on top of him.

"You son-of-a-bitch. You want me to pay for my own suits and you want to make a profit off me!" The guy had gone pale. "Keep the suits," I said, "and good luck finding someone who'll fit 'em."

Not the best way to come home. Not only was I homeless again, but I was suit-less, too. Luckily I had friends like Mickey Clark who offered to let me share an apartment uptown for the next couple of months.

The tour had been fun, but after two months on the road it was good to be back in New York. Before I had gone on tour, I went back into the studio to record four more songs on the Columbia contract. The label planned to release the single three months later with *Crazy Arms*, a crossover country song. In my opinion, Soul and Country together was not the best way to forge an identity and a following.

I was so frustrated with Columbia, that even though I had wanted so badly to get back to New York, all I wanted now was to get away from everyone so I went out to Los Angeles, this time only to stay with my sister Janice, and visit my brothers. I was again at a crossroads. People in California were talking about Las Vegas, so from LA I decided to head to Nevada and check out possible work in Vegas.

In Vegas one night at a new venue called the Pussycat A-Go-Go, I was talking to the manager and telling him about my musical career. He asked me if I wanted to sit in with the band, so when they took their break I talked to them, and decided on a couple of songs to perform. It was an informal audition, but the management went nuts over my performance, and before the night was over I had a two-week booking later that month.

Two star singers preceded me at the Pussy Cat. One was Doby Gray, of *The In Crowd* fame, and the other was Bobby Freeman of *Do You Want to Dance?* fame (or rather "Doo ya, doo ya, doo ya, doo ya wanna dannzzz?"). The club was packed every night, and the audience loved my intensity and high energy.

I called Scandore and Shayne to tell them I was in Vegas. Joe Scandore arranged for me to meet his biggest client, Don Rickles, backstage at one of the big hotels and casinos where Rickles was playing. Known ironically as "Mister Warmth" for his skill at insulting people, backstage Rickles' personality was more like the name of the club where I was playing. His wife, Barbara, was especially polite and friendly, and he offered to get me tickets for his next show. "I'll make sure they got them at the door for you," Rickles said.

"That would be very nice of you, but would it be okay if I brought a date?"

"Sure kid, no problem, I'll arrange it."

My date was a showgirl who was in the *Lido de Paris* cabaret review at the Stardust Hotel. The cabaret was all Parisian decadence, with musical acts and beautiful women in extravagant costumes, some topless. Vegas was all show and neon, but little substance and, as on the Pitney tour, I felt out of place. Vegas just wasn't my scene, and despite how genuine and friendly someone like Don Rickles was, I really wanted to be back in New York recording again; I missed my friends like Mickey Clark.

Then one night one of my friends from New York showed up.

I was on stage at the Pussycat when suddenly a familiar voice came out of the audience. "Who in the hell is that white nigga up there on stage!" the voice yelled.

I looked through the lights, and there coming down the aisle was my old buddy Richard Pryor. We were more than two years removed from our days at the Wha? and in that time Pryor had gone from the slightly awkward and nervous comic I had known, to a major superstar. Pryor ran up on stage with me, and we started jiving as though were still back at the Wha?

"How you doin'?" I asked him.

But Pryor didn't want to talk about himself. Giving me a hug he turned to the audience and told them, "This nigga Turley can sing like no other."

"You know I can't pay you," I said.

"Aaaaah, all you want to do is whip me!"

"You wanta sing?" I asked

"Hell no!"

"You wanta dance?"

"*Hell* no!"

I turned to the audience and said "Hey, you-all ever hear of a colored boy that couldn't sing and dance?"

"Hey! Wait a minute motherfucker! I kick yo ass!"

We gave the unsuspecting but thrilled audience fifteen minutes of stand-up comedy—just two old friends getting caught up.

Then he got serious before he left the stage. He turned to the audience and said, "You know, all kidding aside, this man is one of the best singers you'll ever hear in your lifetime."

Before he left the stage, he leaned over to me and told me he would leave tickets for his show the next night at the door. The next night, after his show we went up to his room where we partied with two showgirls. Then about 2:00 AM, when I thought we were winding down, he said to me, "C'mon Turley, we're going out."

"Where to?"

"Just come with us. I want you to see the most beautiful thing you're ever gonna see."

Pryor had a station wagon and we drove into the desert with the showgirls. It was still dark and the roads were empty and lonely, but Pryor knew where he was going as he drove up into some hills overlooking a valley.

"This is it," he said as he parked the car and got out. From the back of the station wagon he took out some folding chairs and handed them to us. He led us a little way off the road before choosing a spot for us to set up the chairs. Then we sat and waited.

"Richard," I asked him, "what are we doing?"

"Just watch, man. In a few minutes you'll see."

We were facing the east valley. Below us the distant lights of Vegas twinkled.

"Just watch, man," Pryor said again.

I saw what we were waiting for. At first it was just a purplish haze on the horizon, but as a small sliver of the sun came over the mountain, the purple changed to pastels of orange streaked with red, pink, and blue. Below us the desert valley was silent.

"What did I tell you?" Pryor said to me. He sat back in his chair, happy and serene. There was nothing here to disturb him—no crowds, no commitments, and no painful memories.

"You were right," I said. With the universe now in peaceful order, we sat and watched the sunrise. For once, *we* were the audience.

Throughout the years, I've tried to contact Richard to talk with him and catch up, but he has become such a huge star, that I can't penetrate his management. I really wanted to thank him for that sunrise, and let him know how much it meant to me both before and after I went blind. The memory of that morning with the sky full of colors, spent with a good friend has helped me through many dark times.

CHAPTER 11

At the beginning of 1967, I was back in New York. Nothing was happening with Columbia, so I went back to playing the clubs around the city, re-building a following while reconnecting with my old crowd and good friends. The world was changing fast with psychedelia, Sgt. Pepper, The Dead, and the San Francisco hippies. What was new and "in" didn't matter to me because I was still trying to stay loyal to my roots and what I did best.

Changes were coming. First, Columbia dropped me and then I parted with Scandore and Shayne. It was nothing personal, it was just business. You get your shot, and if nothing happens, then it's time to move on. The head of Columbia, Tom Noonan, called me in for a meeting.

"Turley," he said, "we've come to a conclusion after recording eight sides that it's just not happening. We're not going to renew your contract, so you're free to go wherever you want."

I stood up and replied, "Tom, you have to admit that you guys were all over the board trying to decide what style of music you wanted. There's no doubt in my mind that I should have stayed in R&B/Soul. I do thank you so much for giving me the opportunity to record."

We shook hands and I walked out. I wasn't angry, because it was an opportunity and I had made some money. I felt that the company threw away a lot of their money, but it was their company.

I had accumulated plenty of contacts throughout the past three years, so I left Noonan's office and went down to a pay phone in the street. I stood there for a while trying to decide who I should call when I remembered that Jack Wederman had just been named president of Kapp Records. After all, it was Jack who had originally signed me to Columbia. As I spoke to his secretary, I heard Jack call out from his office, "Is that Turley you're talking to? Put him through!"

I explained to Jack what had happened that morning with Columbia. "Idiots," Jack said. "I'll sign you, Turley."

I was dropped by Columbia at 11:00 AM, and by 2:00 that afternoon I was signed with another label. I had turned disappointment into opportunity. Mom had taught me well.

Not everything changed. Paul Tannen, who had been my producer on my Columbia singles, remained an important connection throughout the next two years. Ironically, the first big opportunity Paul got for me, took me right back to the offices of Joe Scandore and Mel Shayne.

Scandore and Shayne represented the Kingsmen, who had scored a monster hit in 1963 with their hit record Louie Louie. In the spring and summer of 1967, the Kingsmen were booked to do a tour but their co-founder, singer, and front man, Lynn Easton, quit the group in early summer. The band and Scandore and Shayne were suddenly in a big financial jam. Canceled shows meant loss of revenue and potential lawsuits for breach of contract from angry promoters. That was when Paul Tannen thought of me.

Turley Richards 1967 promotional photo during the Kingsmen tour.

"Turley is perfect," Paul told Mel Shayne. "He'll be great, and you won't have to cancel the tour."

However, when Paul approached me I wasn't sold.

"The Kingsmen?" I said to Paul. "You know rock isn't my style."

"C'mon Turley, Mel Shayne knows you'd be a great front man, and he wants you."

"Well, unless they want to pay me out the yin-yang, I'm not interested."

Scandore and Shayne were between a rock and a hard place. They made a cash offer that I couldn't refuse, so for the next two months I became a Kingsmen, puttering around in an old tour bus. We played small venues and county fairs for screaming kids across the East, South, and Midwest.

The Kingsmen were good guys and I had a lot of fun, just as I did on the Gene Pitney tour, but there was still that nagging feeling that I was out of place. Here I was, a white soul singer, touring Middle America with a bubble gum rock group, during the psychedelic "summer of love." While Jimi Hendrix (having left behind his napkins and bare feet), was captivating the music world at the Monterrey Pop Festival, or bands like the Grateful Dead and Jefferson Airplane were inviting everyone to Haight-Ashbury for a good time, we were playing in auditoriums and nightclubs off the beaten path.

The money was good, and we made some good memories. The guys in the group dug my singing, and I made the most of the energy from the audience with my physical show on stage. Another benefit of being the band's front man was that I got most of the girls.

"How the hell does he do it?" the other guys would say after the show when another group of girls followed me to the bus.

But sometimes being the so-called "babe-magnet" could get a little dangerous, especially when there was a jealous boyfriend involved. In Atlanta we played at one of the larger clubs on the tour, named "The Kitten Corner," which turned out to be something of a go-go bar with scantily dressed dancers. We played five nights, and I hooked up with a couple of the girls, which caused me to find a gun pointed at my face on our fourth night.

"What do you think people will say when they read about the dead singer in the newspapers?" the guy holding the gun said to me.

"What the hell are you talking about?" I said.

"You've been screwing my fiancé."

The guy was right, I had been; I just didn't know she had a fiancée. But this was one time I thought it best to put aside Sam's advice about always telling the truth.

"No, I haven't."

"Yes you have, and now I'm going to fucking kill you."

"I haven't been with your girl, but if you want to go, then why don't you put that gun down and we can fight it out."

"You've been fucking her, and I'm going to kill you."

"Okay. I haven't been with your girl, but there's nothing I can say to make you believe me, so either fight me or shoot me!"

Surprisingly, the guy lowered the gun. "Okay, I'm gonna check this out, but if I find out it's true then I'll be coming back."

Two days later we moved on, and I hadn't seen him.

That wasn't the only run-in I had with the wrong end of a gun. Shortly after the tour, when I was back in New York, I hooked up with a lady I met one night when I was hanging out at The Back Fence. I swear, I didn't know she was married, but apparently she was because we were "interrupted" one night by her husband while we were in the bedroom of her garden apartment. I know this because when we heard the door opening, she said, "Oh my God, that's my husband!"

"You didn't tell me you were married!"

"Oh yeah, I'm married and you've got to get out of here!"

I grabbed my sandals and clothes and ran—naked—out the side door onto their garden. I took off through the gate of the garden with my sandals in my right hand and my shirt, shorts, and underwear in my left. I was running along the alley with the sandals hitting the side of the fence to keep my bearings. Just before I turned right to head down the street, I heard her husband yell something at me, and then I heard a shot. Good Lord, I was being shot at! I made it around the corner, and then stopped long enough to cover my ass (so to speak) and slip my sandals on.

While I was pulling up my underwear, I noticed they had been "air conditioned" for me—there was a bullet hole in the left cheek! I remember being very glad that my ass hadn't been in it. Sheesh, I really needed to start asking women if they were single!

The summer of love eventually wound down, and we closed the tour by Labor Day at the Minnesota State Fair. I was ready to head back to New York. Before the tour I had signed with Jack Wederman and Kapp records, and I was anxious to get back and start recording again. I had come through in the clutch for the Kingsmen and Mel Shayne, and they asked me to stay on and become a permanent member of the group. I appreciated the offer, but I had to be honest with them—rock 'n' roll just wasn't my thing. They understood, so in the Midwestern heat we parted ways. By mid-September I was back in New York. I was ready to start over.

Once I was settled, I got back to music. I was playing around the city again and, most importantly, I was ready to make a new record. Jack and Kapp records were ready for me, too.

Kapp was founded by David Kapp in 1954. Before it was absorbed by MCA records in the early '70s, its artist list ranged from Louis Armstrong to Cher. Kapp's logo was a drum major's hat, the kind that would have fit perfectly with my mother's drum majorette uniforms for South Charleston High.

When it was time to go into the studio, I learned that Jack Wederman had definite ideas about what he wanted me to do. Jack liked Paul Tannen, and he wanted Paul to remain as my producer. I liked Paul too, however, considering the fact that our previous releases on Columbia went nowhere, I felt that changing producers might be the best direction to take. But Jack wanted Paul.

Everyone knew my strength was R&B, but much to my dismay, Kapp wanted me to go the pop route. Jack's vision for my first Kapp record was along the lines of Gary Puckett and the Union Gap, with full orchestration. I could do it because I could sing virtually any musical style, but it wasn't my style. Jack insisted, both on Paul Tannen and the music he wanted me to make. Since I hadn't had any record success thus far, I couldn't argue, so I did my best to give Kapp what they wanted.

With great reluctance about the musical style, I recorded two sides for Kapp with Paul Tannen producing, *This is My Woman* backed by *Everything's Goin' for Me*. And, as I had feared, we came up short again. When Kapp released the record in early 1968, I was not surprised that it went nowhere. Before I knew it, my time with Kapp was also up. My reservations had proven to be correct about the musical style Kapp wanted. I was once again without a record label, and lacking direction in my professional life. My personal life, however, took a turn for the better.

As we all know, in any good relationship there's little to no room for selfishness, and friends are always ready to help each other. Mickey and Sandy were my two closest friends, and I had helped them get together when I let Sandy use my apartment when she first came to New York. Sandy eventually set herself up with her own apartment and a job at a bridal store, where she became friends with a woman named Diane who modeled for the store. Wanting to do us both a good turn and play matchmaker she introduced us.

It was late 1967 when I started dating Diane who also had a three-year-old son named Richard. We all hit it off, and for about a year everything went well, with trips, family get-togethers, and barbeques with Diane's family. I eventually took Diane and Richard to West Virginia to meet my parents. Mickey and Sandy were together, and I thought maybe it was time for me to think about settling down, too. I was dating a very attractive model, was in a stable relationship, and it felt like a "normal" life.

I was playing a new gig at Malachy's, a pub at 73rd and Lexington, which was the hip place to go. When I was on break one night, a guy came up to me to pay his compliments. He was shit-faced drunk, and slurring his words.

"You're the best damned singer I've ever heard!"

"Well, thank you." I said.

"My name's Jake Butts. Damn! I'm gonna get all of my friends in to hear you!

"Thanks," I said again. "That would be great."

Considering Jake's condition, I didn't expect much, but the guy seemed sincere, and I later learned that he was as good as his word.

Jake was in his late twenties and had come to New York from Carmel, California, to become an actor. A graduate of Stanford, Jake attended the American Academy of Dramatic Arts for a year and a half. Unlike most would-be actors who go to Hollywood or New York to make it, Jake was blessed with wealth and independence because his family owned several car dealerships back in Carmel. More importantly, Jake had a heart as big as his love for friendship, fun, and great music, and it was his network of friends—mostly wealthy twenty-some-things like him—that he brought in to hear me sing.

"Look at this crowd Turley," the owner of Malachy's said to me. "There's got to be at least fifty extra people in tonight."

Jake told his friends who, in turn told their friends, and soon there were lines out the door of people who came to Malachy's to hear "the best damned singer you've ever heard!" Soon the management wanted me playing more nights, and we started calling it "TWT with Turley," meaning Turley played Tuesdays, Wednesdays, and Thursdays. Agents and other artists were coming in to hear me, including Marilyn McCoo and the 5th Dimension, but it was mostly Jake's crowd, which included another friend—Jay Wolpert.

Jay met Jake during their stint together in the Coast Guard. In 1968, Jay returned to New York with the Coast Guard by way of a posting to the Brooklyn Navy Yard where he fell in with the crowd of his old friend Jake Butts. An intelligent and educated guy, Jay competed on the television show *Jeopardy* and became their champion of champions for 1969. A successful career followed writing and producing for television, in both Canada and the United States. Eventually Jay moved into screenwriting, collaborating on the scripts for *The Pirates of the Caribbean* and *The Count of Monte Cristo*. On a personal note, Jay and his wife, Roz, are two of the nicest people I have ever known.

When Jay talked about his friend Jake Butts, he would tell people that "Jake Butts was an intense 'recommender.' Jake was always telling you about this restaurant you had to try or that band you had to hear or this movie you had to see. 'Yeah right, Jake,' you would think. But the kicker was that Jake was almost always right!"

Jay continued, "Jake started telling me about this guy named Turley Richards, saying, 'He's the best damned singer you will ever hear. You have to see this guy!' Typical Jake, and so one night we went down to Malachy's. 'That's Turley over there,' Jake says, and I see this big guy talking with the crowd. Finally, about nine o'clock he goes behind the microphone, says hello to the crowd in a soft Southern drawl, jokes around a bit, and begins to play."

Jay Wolpert says he had no idea that I was almost blind. What struck him instead, that first night, was my voice. He would recall that I would mostly do covers of other artists' songs, but completely in my own way.

Jay would say, "He put in his own sweetness where the original version had rough edges, and he put in his own rough edges when the original was all sweetness." Jay was hooked.

Jay continued, "During intermission Jake introduced me to Turley, and only then did I realize that there was an issue with his vision."

Jay had to then re-assess what he had just seen and heard.

"Turley's confidence and bearing were so impressive. I called my wife that night and must have sounded like Jake—'You've got to come and see this guy!' We'd all come down with everyone we knew. Everyone became a big fan."

But the show stopper, according to both Jay and Jake, was when I sang Bob Dylan's *Just Like a Woman,* and as Jay said, I would make it my own. The place would go dead quiet, with each person hanging on every word.

More importantly, Jay said, "When Turley sang his version of *Just Like a Woman,* every guy who brought a date that night, and some who didn't, ended up getting laid."

I met another good friend around the same time I met Jay and Jake, but this one was outside of Jake's crowd. Paul Michalzik was previously a club boxer with an unsung career in which he had fought more than thirty bouts. Paul was as tough outside of the ring as in, and he was also a black-belt in karate. He had a penchant for wearing new loafers with taps.

The story went that some local so-called "tough guys" picked a fight with Paul outside of a Brooklyn bar one night. It was four against one, but Paul took them on anyway, only to slip in mid-kick on his new shoes and fall on his ass. While they laughed, Paul proceeded to beat their asses anyway, minus his shoes.

I was just as happy to have Paul on my side as I had been to have my cousin Guy and my old friend Cap at Goya guitars. I soon hired Paul to get me to my gigs around the city. When I wasn't playing for Jake and his many friends at Malachy's, I was still at the Back Fence or up the street at the Bitter End. I also played a couple of gigs with Mickey Clark.

In 1968, Paul Tannen was hired by Warner Brothers to head their New York office. Their record label was one of the biggest in the music industry. Knowing I was without a recording deal, Paul immediately called me; in a short time, I had a singles deal with Warner Brothers. It was June of 1968, and I was back on track.

My experience has been that life swings like a pendulum. When something bad happens, I know that the pendulum will swing the other way. Unfortunately, the pendulum swings both ways, and I've watched it go back and forth more times than I can count. I have always tried to find meaning in life and to stay true to myself. I was fortunate to get a lot of help, first from my mother, and then from many close friends. With Warner Brothers, the pendulum had surely swung in my favor. I was singing regularly around the Village and Manhattan, building a dedicated following while gaining new friends. But the pendulum swings both ways.

I was playing basketball in a neighborhood schoolyard three weeks after I signed my new contract with Warner Brothers, when I noticed I couldn't see the basket as well as I usually do. I thought my contact lens was dirty, so I kept taking it out and cleaning it, but that didn't help. After a few days of this I thought I'd better go home to West Virginia to see Dr. Chandler.

Janice happened to be in from California for a visit, so she drove me over to Dr. Chandler's office in Charleston. Dr. Chandler examined me, and then told me to go over to his desk and sit down. He stayed in the testing area with his back to me, and even though I couldn't see him well, I could tell he was struggling to gain his composure. I knew something must be seriously wrong. Finally, he turned and walked over to his desk and sat down. He cleared his throat several times and as his eyes welled up with tears as he told me:

"Richard, this is tearing my heart out. I've known you since you were five years old, and I don't know how to tell you this." He stopped.

"Dr. Chandler," I said, "you've always told me things straight, so tell me what it is. I can handle it."

"This is so hard, Richard," he said, his voice cracking. He took another deep breath and said, "You have glaucoma, and it's the worst case I've ever seen." He stopped, and took another deep breath, "You're going to be blind, probably within six to eight months. I'm so sorry."

I felt as if I had been kicked in the stomach, but then my macho side took over. I stood up and jutted my chin out. "Dr. Chandler," I said, "blindness done picked the wrong mother-fucker to fuck with!"

Dr. Chandler wiped his eyes and managed a small laugh. "Richard, I knew I wouldn't have to worry about you."

I walked out of the doctor's office in a total fog, but by the time I reached Janice, my face was composed.

"What did Dr. Chandler say?" she asked. She put her hand on my arm, "Are you all right, Richard?"

I told her, and Janice broke down crying.

When we got back to my parent's house I took Mom by the hand and sat her down on the couch.

"I have some bad news, but we've been through a lot together, Mom"

With tears in her eyes, she looked at me and said, "You're going to go blind, aren't you, honey?"

Janice came into the room and Mom and Janice cried together while I sat on the couch with my arm around each of them. I was too busy consoling my mother and sister to cry myself.

"I'll be okay, don't worry about me," I kept saying. "I'll figure things out. Just don't worry."

My dad had left the room, and that was okay because I knew he needed to do his grieving in private.

The next two days with my family was a period of mourning. I was slowly absorbing and trying to make sense of Dr. Chandler's words: "You'll be blind probably within six to eight months."

"Why?" I wondered, and why now? What was I going to do? At first my biggest concerns weren't about my singing or new contract or even my career.

"I'll never be able to play basketball or shoot pool again," I kept thinking. I was going to lose that part of me—the part I had always considered as my real identity. "Turley" only existed because of Richard's limitations. Richard was the jock and I believed he was the real man; soon he would be gone. A part of me—the real me—was going to die. Were they irrational thoughts? Probably, but they were also probably normal thoughts given the circumstances. Eventually I came to a decision, and made the only choice I thought was reasonable.

"I'm going back to New York," I told my mother.

"But you can't!" my mother cried.

"I have to go back. New York is where my life is, and I have a new record deal, so money is not a problem. I can't stop living."

"But how will you take care of yourself?"

"I'll figure it out. I'll have to. Mickey and Sandy are there, and so is Paul. I have a lot of friends who can help. Mom, if I stay here, what'll happen to me? I'll be living in the upstairs bedroom and you'll be bringing my meals to me and I'll wind up a three-hundred-pound shut-in."

"But . . ."

"No, you know I'm right. I have to go back. What have you always taught me? You always told me that it's a tough world, and that I have to be tougher than the toughest. Remember, Mom: *defeat is no option.*"

"But . . ."

End of argument. She knew I was right.

Glaucoma is a condition caused by the buildup of water behind the eye. Eventually the pressure becomes so great that the optic nerve is damaged. There is no cure for glaucoma, and the best that can be done is to try to slow its progress. Blindness is inevitable.

Dr. Chandler arranged for me to see another specialist in New York. Our goal was to alleviate the pressure behind my right eye so that I could hold off blindness for as long as possible. This would require the right medications. The first attempt was an eye drop. I was laid out on a table and the doctor's assistant got almost on top of me to put the drops in my eye. There was instant and searing pain, as if he had put acid in my eye.

"Oh my god!" I yelled.

Out of pure reflex, I threw up my arms to grab my eye, and the poor little assistant, who was still hovering over me, went flying across the room.

The guy screamed, "He tried to kill me!" as he picked himself off the floor. Apparently eye drops weren't going to work.

The glaucoma had progressed so far and my condition was so precarious that abnormally high doses of medication were required just to keep it from getting worse. With medication, the swelling and pressure were barely brought under control.

When I was in Charleston, Dr. Chandler had told me, "You came to me just in time. The pressure behind your eye is becoming so great that you were literally in danger of your eye blowing out its socket."

Not a pretty picture, and it didn't happen, but the high doses of meds had awful side effects. Since the idea was to reduce the water building behind my eye, the fluids that my body retained needed to be removed, and this meant using massive doses of diuretics that kept me going to the bathroom almost constantly. It was as if I had a tube running straight from my mouth to the other end. It was more than a little inconvenient during the day, and robbed me of sleep at night. Even worse were the tingling sensations I would get at the tips of my fingers, as if they were asleep. When I pressed my fingers down on the fret board of my guitar, the pain was tremendous, as if I were pressing on razor blades instead of strings. Playing the guitar was difficult and painful, but for the time being, I thought, I would just have to deal with it. I believed I had gotten lucky and had avoided worse. What I didn't realize, was that the pendulum hadn't fully swung yet.

CHAPTER 12

Nothing had ever been easy for me, whether it was reading, seeing faces, or shooting a basketball. It was a struggle to grow up this way, but it was also a blessing because even before the age of five, I had never known the world any other way. The way I grew, learned, and moved about was normal to me, and with my mother's unending encouragement I wouldn't be held back from living. "Defeat is no option," she told me. However, my independence would, in many ways, eventually come to an end. A time would come when I would have to learn to accept help and to rely on others to do the things most of us, including myself, took for granted.

I asked Paul Michalzik to do me a favor. Paul had already begun driving me to my gigs and giving me rides wherever I needed to go. Paul definitely had a crazy side to him, which I was witness to (and victim of). When he picked me up at the airport one time on his motorcycle, it was the most terrifying ride of my life, but Paul had a lot of fun. Actually, it was a thrill, and mostly a good time. This time I was asking him to give me a ride for a different purpose. It was October 1968, and I wanted Paul to drive me north of the city where the leaves were turning color. I was told by Dr. Chandler that by his estimation I would be blind by the New Year. If he was right, then this would be the last fall I would ever see, and I wanted to see the colors so I could remember them.

Paul drove me about fifty miles out of New York City, and dropped me off near the woods. I walked around a bit, picking up leaves and looking at their shades and colors. I also thought a lot about the future, about who I was, and who I would have to become. The struggle between Richard and Turley surfaced. Turley was distraught, but it was Richard, or rather my mom, Silba, who eventually took over, and there was suddenly no room for self-pity.

Seeing the leaves helped me recognize some colors, but it wasn't enough. I needed more detail, so I went to an art supply store on 23rd Street. When I walked in I said, "Would you show me where the crayons and paper are?"

"Crayons are over there," answered the woman behind the counter.

"I'm sorry, but I'm almost blind, could you show it to me?"

"Of course I could," she answered. "Do your children like to draw?"

"No," I said, "the crayons are for me. "I've found out that I have glaucoma, and I'll be blind in a few months. I need the crayons so I can study them, to remember the colors."

"Oh," said the woman. I caught the hesitation in her voice. I heard the sudden sympathy that I didn't want, but knew I would have to learn to live with.

"I'm sorry," she said. She helped me find the crayons and a legal pad. "I'm very sorry," she repeated as I paid her, and left the store.

I had been living in New York City for the past four years. Nine years had passed since my first visit with Don Hickson, when I was just a naïve young man. It was nine years since I had "seen the stars."

I had achieved notoriety, and I had a loyal following in the Manhattan and Greenwich Village clubs. I had recorded an album and several singles for four major labels, and I had just signed a new recording contract with Warner Brothers. I was also going blind.

A city like New York, affords many opportunities, and people flock there every day to succeed. It is also easy to become anonymous and fade into the background. If I didn't want to become lost in the crowd, I was going to have to learn to live with other people's reactions to my blindness with grace and dignity. With my fighter mentality and need to be independent, this would likely be a difficult task.

When I got back to my apartment with my crayons and tablet, I immediately went to work. Tilting each crayon, I would eye the colors with a magnifying glass, memorizing the name, and scribbling the color across the paper. When done, I wrote the name of the color across the top, and thumb tacked them to the walls at eye level. When I finished, I got really close and walked from page to page memorizing the colors. It suddenly hit me why I had to do this, and in a rare moment of weakness, I sat on the couch and cried. Soon I would never see these colors again. Every day after that, I worked on imbedding the colors into my memory.

A couple of weeks later someone was visiting me and asked, "What's with all this scribbling on the walls?" When I told her, she reacted with, "Aww," a sound laced with pity.

That angered and embarrassed me, so after she left, I tore them all down and threw them away. The "pity-pot" has never fit me. I needed to move on.

Seeing details at a distance was slowly becoming impossible, so I developed a plan for moving around the city. I quickly learned that I couldn't trust the average New Yorker to actually look at the number on a building when I asked "is this number 234?" Many of them would glance at it and say yes, but I would knock on the door, only to find I was at the wrong place.

Some would give a big New York smile and laugh, "What are ya, blind or something?"

I would laugh and say, "Actually, I am almost blind. Would you please look at the building and tell me the address?" Lesson learned.

Travelling long distances up- or downtown required that I hail a cab, which was usually easier than one might think. This was one area where I was able to hold onto my independence. I would come out of my building, walk across the wide sidewalk, and step off the curb. If I didn't step in dog poop, I knew it was going to be a good day. I would then face the traffic, and hold my hand up and whistle.

A few months after I got back from South Charleston I was playing one of my regular nights at Malachy's. It was a Turley Richards crowd of fans who came out specifically to hear me sing. It was a typical night, with me talking and joking with the crowd between songs. A fan requested Glen Campbell's *By the Time I get to Phoenix*, which was a big hit at the time, but I really disliked it.

I started the song, and then suddenly without warning my voice gave out. At first, I thought maybe my voice just refused to sing the song. Again, I tried to sing, and nothing came out but air. I stopped and took a drink of water and tried to start again, but still nothing. I couldn't sing. I tried to talk, but I couldn't speak either. I felt totally helpless, and thought, "What now?"

I realized there was not a sound in the room, and I felt everyone staring at me. It was as if time had stopped. Finally, I reached over and turned off the PA. I felt everyone watching me as I slipped my guitar into its bag and zipped it up. I stood up, and slung it over my shoulder, and then made my way through the crowd toward the door. These were my fans, who already knew that I was going blind, and they watched me walk through them in helpless disbelief. Several asked if they could help me as I passed by them, but I waved them off.

I headed down Lexington Avenue toward 21st Street and my apartment. I had fifty blocks to cover and an hour's lonely walk to think about what had happened. I was going blind, and now I couldn't sing. First Richard and now Turley were both being erased. What was I going to do now? I kept walking, and as I walked, I became more and more angry. I finally made it to my apartment, where I set aside my guitar and stripped off my shirt in anger and frustration. I needed to make sense of this. Something, someone, must be to blame.

I had never before thought about God, the one belief of my mother's that had never rubbed off. His existence or lack thereof had never held any importance. But now I was desperate for meaning.

Finally, in bitterness, I unzipped my pants and grabbed my crotch and I looked up at the ceiling. "Here!" I rasped, "You've taken my eyes, now you've taken my voice, why don't you just take this too while you're at it!"

The next thing I knew, the phone was ringing with the high, jangly sound of the old rotary phone. Slowly I became aware of it and came to, looking and feeling around to get my bearings.

I started and yelled, *"Oh fuck!"* I was sitting on a window sill in my apartment. The window was open with my legs hanging over the edge of the seven-story drop to 7th Avenue. It was still dark outside and the street was empty. I was stark naked. My clothes were lying in a pile in the middle of the floor, and the phone was ringing.

"What!" I croaked into the phone.

"Hey man, you want a good bet tomorrow?"

"Do I what?"

"Bet. I got a good one at Belmont tomorrow. Twenty to one—can't miss."

"You got the wrong fucking number—forget it!"

I hung up the receiver and looked around the room. Then it all came rushing back—losing my voice, the long walk home, stripping off my shirt, then grabbing myself and yelling at God. But why was I naked, and how did I wind up on the window sill? I guess I will never know.

I checked the time and saw it was just after 2:00 AM. I had left Malachy's around 10:00, and it had taken me about an hour to walk home, so that left about three hours I couldn't account for. Had I been sitting on the window sill the entire time? What was I thinking about and why didn't I remember any of it? That was the scary part. I looked up at the ceiling, and I started to relax a little. But then I suddenly remembered what I had yelled at the ceiling and at God...

"Oh shit," I thought, and I grabbed my crotch. To my relief, and then amusement, everything was still there. I smiled, and my crisis passed. I was thankful to be alive.

That night at Malachy's still haunts me. There are so many questions and so many should-have-beens in my life that stretch all the way back to when I was hit with the arrow. Today I still try to make sense of it all. From a curious look back at the wrong moment, to the wrong doctor, and then the right one. From a supportive mother who helped me learn about choices and overcoming limits to a rollercoaster career. Finally, yet another new start, only to end with what may have always been inevitable—going blind. But to lose my voice along with everything else? What had kept me on that window ledge for three hours? There has to be a reason for it all.

The medical reason for losing my voice was soon found, and it was the glaucoma medication. My dosage was so high that it was dehydrating me, and it had finally affected my throat and voice. The meds were adjusted, and my voice recovered. There would be other side effects to deal with, but my singing, my identity, and meaning had returned.

That night at Malachy's was intense and frightening, and made me consider a lot of what ifs. What if I did lose my voice? What if I had jumped from that open window or accidently fallen? What if I had never looked back? What if I was capable of doing something like that in the future? The last one was my biggest fear.

In the following days I tried to make sense of it in a song, *Tomorrow Will Never Come*. Simple but powerful, the lyrics poured out of me in a rush:

> *The neon lights are dim tonight through my window.*
> *The stars are broken and the moon is hiding in the shadows.*
> *The sky is black, the wind is cold, and the rain's pounding like a drum.*
> *But, what do I care; tomorrow will never come.*
> *Well, it's too late now, for me to start all over again,*
> *I'm so tired of trying and sick with crying through this phony grin*
> *And I know for me, there'll never be, another shining sun.*
> *But, what do I care, tomorrow will never come.*
> *Tomorrow will never come . . .*

In the lyrics I've lost hope and meaning of my life, but in the end I never have. I always keep going—rekindling hope and looking for new meaning.

So what had kept me in that window? Fate? Luck? God? Different theories have been put to me throughout the years. My clinical friends say it was my subconscious will to live (our most basic instinct) that kept me from jumping or falling. Others have called it "dissociation," and say it happened because my brain, trying to cope with the stress and trauma I was experiencing, shut me down and saved my life. That would also explain why I blacked out.

That's the clinical explanation, but it's also been put to me that there was perhaps a more profound reality that saved me that night. In my distress and time of need I called out to be saved. If that's true, then I did it in a pretty unconventional way. What about the phone call, asking if I wanted to place a bet? Was it random, or was it meant to wake me up and save my life? God may work in mysterious ways, but with me, He must have a special sense of humor. Most people are saved by an angel, but instead I get a call from God's bookie.

CHAPTER 13

As I said, to my great relief my voice came back and I continued to play around town at different clubs. During a break one night at Malachy's, I was approached by a woman from Phoenix, who introduced herself as Julia Motta. She told me she was in town for the Westminster Dog Show. She wanted me to sing for a private party she was hosting while she was in town.

"I really love your singing! Would you consider coming over to our hotel tomorrow night and singing for everyone? My budget only allows me to pay you $1,000, but what I can do to make up the difference, is give you a beautiful Rhodesian Ridgeback puppy."

"Well, I've been thinking about getting a dog, but what's a Rhodesian Ridgeback?"

"They're an African breed, and worth up to $2,000. I know a breeder in New York."

"What size are these dogs?" I asked

"Females get to 70 or 80 pounds, but males grow to 90 or 110 pounds."

Without hesitation I answered, "As long as it's a male, I'm in."

I went to Julia's hotel to perform the next night and had a chance to meet some of their dogs; I fell in love with them. She gave me the name of a Ridgeback breeder in New Paltz, New York, named Barbara Briggs. A few weeks later, I went up to her kennel with Diane to see the dogs. Barbara had six or seven puppies huddled together in a pen. As we approached them and he heard my voice, one puppy's head popped up, and he ran ahead of the others. My arm was in the pen by then, and he jumped on it, wrapping his legs around me.

"I guess he picked you!" Barbara said.

You bet he did.

According to the dog breeder's registry for Ridgebacks, the names for Barbara Briggs' litter were designated to all start with a "K." The name for my new puppy was Kiongazi, which is Swahili for "leader." I would own other dogs through my life, but I would never have another one with truer loyalty and a better temperament.

Ridgebacks are striking dogs, not just for their size but also for their regal bearing. Kion was never meant to be a guide dog because that's not why I wanted a dog. I do believe that having something to take care of and be responsible for helped me adjust to blindness. Kion needed me, and I desperately needed that.

I would often take him to Central Park to run. To get to the park, Kion and I would stop at the curb where I would tell Kion to "stay." Leaning forward, ready to run we would wait while I tilted my head to listen for traffic. If I didn't hear any cars, I would yell *"Okay!"* and we would take off running to the other side. We covered four blocks this way, just a couple of big kids playing in traffic!

We were in the park one day, when suddenly all of the other dogs began running toward the road. The other dog owners started screaming and running after them.

"Is my dog with them?" I asked one of the other owners. He was, so I asked her to point my finger in his direction. Four short whistles and she said, "Your dog stopped and is looking at you."

"Place!" I yelled, pointing down at a spot next to me.

To the astonishment of everyone, Kion took one last longing look at his would-be buddies, turned, and then ran the several hundred yards back to me and sat down by my side.

Kion was loyal and protective, and had interesting and funny ways of taking out his revenge on those he didn't like. New York had a quarantine law concerning new dogs, which restricted their movements outdoors for their first two weeks.

Since my apartment didn't allow dogs, Kion and I wound up moving in with an acquaintance until the quarantine was up, and I could find an apartment that accepted pets.

The roommate didn't like Kion, and yelled at him often for doing the things that puppies do. Because of that, Kion didn't like him either.

Early one morning, the roommate, who chose to never wear socks with his boots, woke me up with his scream, *"That goddamn dog!"*

I jumped out of bed and went to the hallway to ask what had happened.

"Holy shit, Turley, your dog crapped in my boot!" My roommate was furious, and asked me to leave as soon as the quarantine was over. Luckily we only had four days left.

Kion was also a great guard dog. I had moved into a new apartment uptown on 94th and Lexington. Kion and I were lying on the floor one night watching television, when he started to whine. He jumped up, ran to the bedroom window, and then I heard him growl. A burglar had unlatched the window and was crawling in. Kion charged him, knocking him out of the window to the balcony below. When the police arrived, they found the guy still lying on his back with me standing over him. He couldn't move, and the police had to take him to the hospital before they could take him to jail.

Kion was the last thing I ever saw, and he was my best friend for thirteen years.

Warner Brothers Records was a label as big and prestigious as Columbia. Their artist list included Van Morrison, who was at the top of his game in the late '60s. The label would eventually run through some the biggest names in the '70s, including the monster-selling Fleetwood Mac. Paul Tannen wanted me to make a demo for Warner, and on the strength of the demo he got me my singles deal. Once again, I was all set for a new start.

Paul's first idea was for us to go down to Nashville to record my first single for Warner Brothers. I liked the idea, and thought that musically we could do something interesting. Paul booked the sessions, and we were ready to go. The two titles would be *Tomorrow Will Never Come,* the song I wrote after that night at Malachy's when I lost my voice and came to on my window ledge. I still couldn't remember much about that night, and it haunted me.

The second title we chose was *Freedom Mountain.* I was proud of *Freedom Mountain* and thought it was a great song. It was 1969, the world was filled with political and social protest, and in my lyrics I was starting to reflect the times and the world around me.

In the middle of all this upheaval, we all took time out to watch two of my best friends join their lives in marriage.

On March 29, 1969, my good friend Mickey Clark married his girlfriend, Sandy. Both were from Louisville, Kentucky, the city I would one day call home. Mickey had casually suggested that Sandy move to New York, after she complained about her job. Like everyone who's ever gone to New York, she was looking for a new start.

I met Sandy through Mickey in Louisville, and when I heard that she wanted to make the move I offered her my apartment for the two months when I would be away on the Kingsmen tour. Not worrying about a place to stay allowed her to get used to the city and land a job.

That's what friends do for each other. And two years later, Mickey asked me to be his best man at their wedding. By the spring of '69, I was in the middle of the many transitions that would change my life, some hopeful, some painful, but Mickey and Sandy's wedding was a happy day.

The wedding ceremony took place at St. Monica's Church on 79th Street, and then we all headed for a small but fun reception at the Madison Café, known as Harry's Bar to the regulars, on Madison Avenue. It was a musician's wedding, so naturally there would be music. As the Best Man I was asked to sing, and Mickey's friend Ian Tyson of the folk singing duo Ian and Sylvia, would sing too. Ian and Mickey sang the hit Ian had with Sylvia, titled *Four Strong Winds,* and then I played a set that included *Just Like a Woman.* I figured if it got the response that Jay always said it did, Mickey was sure to get laid on his wedding night. Lastly, I shared the stage with Ian Tyson, exchanging one-liners like musicians do, which got a lot of laughs from the crowd.

Diane was there, and others said that we made a handsome couple. Today, when people look at the pictures of the wedding and reception, they describe seeing a group of happy young men and women.

However, the happiness that Diane and I had was not to last. I can say that something happened that summer of '69 but I won't say what it was. Suffice it to say that along with the trauma of going blind, everything changed between us.

Telling my story has resulted in recalling long buried memories of the three years from 1968 to 1971 that ended in my total blindness. Unfortunately, I was so wrapped up in my own fear and pain that I just drifted away from Diane without ever talking to her about what was happening. I probably did this to other people in my life too. I felt a great need to tackle blindness alone, almost as if it were a one-on-one basketball game. In the end, I just didn't have enough energy left over for a personal relationship. I also truly felt that Diane and her son would be better off not being pulled into the vacuum of my blindness.

It was June of 1969, and I had been signed to Warner Brothers Records for almost a year when the label's president, Mike Maitland, heard me sing one night at the Bitter End. Maitland loved what he heard and came backstage afterward to introduce himself.

"Turley," Maitland said, "that was incredible. You've got one of the best voices I've ever heard. Tell me, when's your album coming out?"

"Well," I answered, "I don't have an album deal."

"You gotta be kidding!" Maitland said. "Turley, you come in to the office here on Monday, and we'll give you an album deal. Consider it done."

When we met on Monday, I learned there was another condition that Mike wanted, "Paul and I were discussing the deal, and we decided you need a new producer, and we want it to be a two album deal."

By now Paul Tannen had been my producer with three different labels. If Paul was disappointed by what he and Mike Maitland had agreed upon, he never let on, and soon he was connecting me with one of the top record producers of the time, Lew Merenstein. Lew and I sat in his office for two or three hours listening to songs, and together we chose eight songs, including four of my own, and two each by Bob Dylan and Gordon Lightfoot. We left the possibility of a ninth song open. Over the next few months, we would record the album at Mirror Studios in New York.

My personal and professional relationships had changed quickly over the past year. During 1969, I had a new contract with Warner Brothers. Through Paul Tannen, I had a new producer in Lew Merenstein, and through Lew I met my new manager, Bob Schwaid. Bob, along with Marty Thau, formed the production company Schwaid-Merenstein & Thau.

I met Schwaid one day when I went to see Lew Merenstein in his office. Lew wanted me to meet the members of the company and introduced me first to Marty Thau. Marty was on his way out of the office, so we only had time for a quick hello. Lew introduced me to Schwaid, who at the time was managing Van Morrison and the international singing star Miriam Makeba. Bob made it plain that he wanted to sign me, and after a few meetings over dinner I agreed to let him become my third manager.

I hadn't worked with a manager in nearly two years, but with my career about to take off, I thought it was a good idea to have one again. Since Bob was a partner of Lew Merenstein's it seemed natural to sign with him. It was through Bob Schwaid and his connections at ICM that in 1970, I did the most extensive touring of my career.

While my sighted world narrowed, my professional world was expanding. By 1969 I had moved from William Morris to International Creative Management (ICM), and began to work outside of New York City. Accompanied by Paul Michalzik across New York State and Boston, I was opening for such acts as the First Edition with Kenny Rogers, Neil Diamond, my old friend from the Wha? Richie Havens, Joni Mitchell, and comedians Shelly Burman and George Carlin.

After one of our shows, Richie Havens said, "You always knock me out, man. It's just a matter of time."

Through ICM, I was also starting to sing on national television shows such as David Frost, Dick Cavett, Merv Griffin, Dave Garroway, and Mike Douglas. I was backstage on the *Mike Douglas Show* with Joan Rivers, actor Van Johnson, and the great opera singer Robert Merrill, when Merrill asked me where I had taken lessons.

"Um, nowhere," I said, a little shocked by his sudden praise. "I just bang hard on my guitar."

"No," Merrill said, "I'm not talking about your guitar; I'm talking about your singing."

When I told him that I had never had a vocal lesson, Merrill turned to the others in the room and said, "I don't know if you believe in God or not, but this young man has been blessed with perfect fundamentals."

I was honored to have this high praise from such a great talent.

Every talk show has a waiting lounge, which is commonly known as the "green room." It's usually filled with an unlikely collection of performers who mostly keep to themselves. The crew are very helpful, though, and the atmosphere is relaxed. Typically we were given a few minutes to set up or do a sound check before the show, and then we waited in the green room for our call. Sometimes if a guest ran over time, we might get "bumped" and never make the appearance.

My biggest television break came in the fall of '69 with an appearance on the *Tonight Show* with Johnny Carson. With a nightly audience of up to sixteen million viewers, Carson had already earned his title "The King of Late Night." This was before Carson moved the *Tonight Show* from New York to Los Angeles. As far as network primetime prestige went, it was the show to be on.

I was scheduled to appear on the *Tonight Show* a few weeks earlier but was "bumped" when the talkative actor Tony Randall went way over his allotted time. Whether Randall was that interesting or Carson was just being polite I can't recall. What I do remember were the angry rumbles from the other guests in the green room who were waiting to go on. "Somebody shut that SOB up!" and "Get him the hell off!" were their frustrated complaints. Finally Randall stopped, but it was too late for me.

The second time around, in the green room before the show, I found myself with the usual improbable mix, from comedian Woody Allen to acting icons Gwenn Verdon and William Holden. Making some friendly small talk I was telling Allen about my new dog, when Holden overheard our conversation.

"Excuse me," Holden began, "were you saying that you owned a Ridgeback?"

It turned out that in his spare time, Holden was a big game safari hunter. During his many trips to Africa, he came to own several Rhodesian Ridgebacks, which were a fairly rare breed of dogs in the States at the time. Safari hunting and Ridgebacks were two passions that Holden loved to talk about, and he asked me if I'd like to catch dinner with him after the show.

"Sure, Mr. Holden," I said. "My mother would kill me if I didn't have dinner with you; she's a big fan of yours."

Even as I said this I cringed inside. "My mother's a big fan," ouch! That's like someone coming up to me today and saying that their grandma loved my version of *Just Like a Woman*.

A few minutes before I went on I was directed to the stage where I had done my sound check. Sitting on a stool I waited for Carson's introduction. Was I nervous? The simple answer was no, not at all. Singing was my life's blood, and maybe I was a cocky SOB, but by the late sixties, I was also a pro. I knew it was my big shot, but I wasn't nervous about the performance itself. To me, singing on television was just the same as if I was in front my usual crowd at Malachy's or The Bitter End.

"This next young man you're about to meet," Carson began in his crisp Nebraska accent, "came to the attention of our staff at a recent audition. He'll be appearing shortly at the Bistro in Columbus, Ohio, and was just signed for two weeks at Mister Kelly's in Chicago opening on November 17. This is his first network television appearance, will you make him feel welcome please, Turley Richards . . ." Applause . . . and I'm *on*.

I remember the same line running through my head that I always thought right before a basketball game: "This is it, big guy. Now get out there and do your thang."

I had decided to perform Gershwin's *Summertime* for the show. I was in great voice that night, and at the end of the song, I hit an enormously long, falsetto note, that I was told brought the audience to their feet. Years later, I was doing a corporate show with the first host of the *Tonight Show*, Steve Allen. Allen told me that my ovation that night was one of the longest standing ovations *The Tonight Show* ever had for a singer. All I knew was that I had accomplished what I wanted, and in those very short yet timeless three minutes, I had made my impression.

When Carson himself stopped clapping he turned back to the audience and the cameras, "I think you may hear a lot from that young man," Carson said, "Turley Richards!"

"Performing on The Tonight Show was truly one of the great highlights of my career."

CHAPTER 14

The sixties were closing out. In the summer of '69, Vietnam was at its peak, we landed a man on the Moon, Woodstock (where my friend Richie Havens performed) captivated the country, and the New York Mets won the World Series. And I was going blind. I was working hard to keep moving forward, so I guess it was "the perfect storm" when Adrian Nutter walked into Malachy's one night toward the end of the year. Adrian was an aspiring model from Long Island who was working as a waitress. She seemed supportive, and I needed support through this difficult time. Adrian usually got what she wanted, and Adrian wanted me. We began dating, and shortly after that, Adrian showed up at my door asking to move in "for a few days." She had been sharing a place with a girlfriend, but when they got into an argument, she lost both her roommate and her apartment. And so she came to me with her suitcases of clothes and her record collection. She even had a dog. I got a beautiful live-in girlfriend, and Kion also got a new friend to play with in Central Park. It worked out for both of us—for a while. But we'll get back to her later.

"Blindness has picked the wrong motherfucker to fuck with," I had told Dr. Chandler, and I was trying my best to live up to my shout of defiance; but I was also human. When I was around my friends like Mickey, Jake, Jay, and Paul, I tried to stay upbeat. Superman was just fine. Inside, though, and in private, I was having trouble dealing with what lay ahead of me, and with what I was leaving behind.

I became very sensitive to the sights and sounds of things that I had loved, the things that I thought defined who I was. If I was walking past a school yard or basketball court, and heard the sounds of dribbling, it would hit me. If I was in a bar and heard the sounds of a pool game, it would hit me. If I saw a television ad for this or that organization for the blind it would hit me. I was still only in my late twenties, and I thought blindness was going to rob me of being a man. I wouldn't be able to play basketball or shoot pool, and women wouldn't find me attractive. Instead, I would become an object of sympathy or worse, pity. It was too much, and it must have begun to show because it was Paul who eventually became my mirror—the kind of mirror that showed the unflattering image of what I had become.

"Goddamn it, Turley!" Paul yelled at me one day in my apartment, "Where is the Turley that made us all laugh? You've disappeared! For God's sake, you're six foot four and 215 pounds of solid muscle! There's no way you look like a pitiful guy tapping a cane down the damn street. I've had it!" Paul stormed out and slammed the door behind him, leaving me alone.

I walked up to a big mirror I had, put my face close to the glass, and then said to my image, "You know he's right." I decided right then to stop my slide downward. "Life's always been a two-way street," I said to myself, "but now it's only one way." Paul was right, there was no going back, and from that day forward, I made a conscious effort to make people laugh (or at least smile).

In the fall of '69 I still had some sight left, but barely. To control my glaucoma, even at this advanced stage, I was still taking extreme doses of medication. Although they had been adjusted so that my voice could return, I was plagued by side effects such as the tingling and pain in the fingers of my left hand when I played my guitar. I was also extremely dehydrated, and would get chronic stomach aches from the dehydration. Both became so acute at times that I would wind up in a hospital emergency room every seven to eight weeks. There was nothing I could do about the pain except to deal with it, and soon I was off to Columbus with Paul Michalzik. From Columbus we would head out to Chicago and the famous Jazz club, Mister Kelly's, where I would be opening for the soon to be legendary comedian George Carlin.

On our way to Chicago, my stomach pain became almost too much to deal with. I didn't dare stop taking my medication, so I had to try to treat the pain myself. Paul stopped the car and went into a store coming out with two bottles of stuff that promised to relieve stomach pain. I took it immediately, and because it helped some, I kept taking it over the next two days. At our hotel, a friend visiting my room noticed the two empty bottles and saw that there was a serious problem.

"Turley," she asked, "have you been drinking this stuff?"

"Yeah," I said. "It's for my stomachache. Why?"

"Because there's a glaucoma warning label on it! You can't drink this!"

Paul jumped out of his chair and grabbed the bottles in a panic. "Oh my god, Turley! What the fuck have I done? What the fuck have I done to you!"

The medicine Paul bought did indeed have the warning label on it, and the consequence if ignoring it was deteriorated vision. For me, that meant blindness would come sooner. Paul was beside himself, but I couldn't blame Paul, and I didn't want him blaming himself. After all, we were strong young guys—the ex-boxer and superman. We didn't have to read warning labels—that was for ordinary mortals and old people. When dehydration had briefly taken my voice, I probably had been warned about drinking enough water with my meds, but did I listen? Paul had bought the bottles, but it was my responsibility to remind him to check the labels too, and I hadn't. Like most guys our age, we thought that we were invincible and that made us a little reckless. But Paul was still horrified at what he thought he had done.

"Oh my god, Turley, I've caused you to go blind!"

"No you haven't," I said. "You're not making me go blind. That was decided a long time ago, and you had nothing to do with it. I've got 5 percent vision left, so now it's going to go down to 2 percent. So what? It's all inevitable Paul, and it's not your fault."

I was never sure if Paul entirely accepted this, but I was sincere and meant what I said—it wasn't his fault. I truly loved Paul, and he was a great friend. My vision did greatly deteriorate right after that incident, but a few weeks later, I had an experience that has given me one of my favorite funny stories of all time.

I was headed to the studio one day to record the album with Lew Merenstein, and needed to hail a cab. I felt something stop in front of me. It seemed too big to be a cab, but I couldn't figure out what it was.

A deep voice called out to me, "What the hell you doin'?"

"I'm trying to get a cab," I said.

Again came the booming voice, "This is a goddamn garbage truck."

"Sorry," I said, "I'm almost blind, and I'm too proud to ask for help."

"Wait a minute, man." I heard the truck door open.

Now, I'm six feet, four inches, but this black dude towered over me. It felt like I was in front of a mountain that blocked out the sun.

"For God's sake, how tall are you?" I asked.

He answered, "I'm six feet, ten inches and about 420 pounds. Name's Mark. Who are you?"

"My name's Turley."

"Turley, lemme get you a cab. Wait right here."

Mark turned and stepped off the curb.

"*Taxi!*" he yelled. I heard what sounded like twenty cars screeching to halt.

"*You!*" I heard him order. "Pull over!"

A yellow cab did as it was told and pulled up in front of us. Mark came back and helped me to the back door of the cab and I got in.

"Now where you goin,' Turley?" he asked me, with his enormous face filling my window.

"54th and 7th," I answered.

Mark transferred his face to the driver's window. "How much this gonna cost, my brother?"

"About five dollars," the driver said.

Mark straightened up and spoke to me, "I'll be right back, Turley." He pointed his finger at the driver, "Don't move!"

He walked away, and came back a moment later with a pen and paper. Leaning through the back window he took down the driver's cab number and name. Then he wrote down his own name and phone number, tore that part from the pad, and handed it to me.

"Here's my name and phone number. I got his, so if this ride costs more than five bucks, you call me, all right?"

"Thanks, man," I said. I put out my hand and he shook it, with a hand so big it felt like two hands wrapped around my own.

The cabbie pulled away and we headed downtown. I listened for the sound of the meter arm being pulled down, but didn't hear it . . ."

"Aren't you going to put down the meter?" I asked.

"Hell *no!* You think I want King Kong commin' after me?"

That made me laugh really hard, and I agreed with him saying, "Man, that was one big dude."

The cabbie sounded like a little old black man, and I felt for him, so I gave him the five bucks anyway. When we arrived at the studio to meet Lew, the cabbie got out and walked me to the door. As I shook his hand good-bye, he said, "Now, don't you be callin' him!" We both laughed.

As I walked away, I thought Mark was a nice man. So far, most of my experiences with asking for help were turning out pretty well . . . and pretty funny.

Lew Merenstein started in music as a recording engineer. When Paul introduced us in 1969, Lew had already made his name in the music industry, and was just coming off producing Van Morrison's legendary album *Astral Weeks*. His impressive resume included the following great artists: The Spencer Davis Group, The Mamas and the Papas, Miriam Makeba, and Curtis Mayfield.

One of the Dylan songs Lew wanted me to record was *Love Minus Zero—No Limit*. He played Joan Baez's cover version for me. I didn't like the song, but Lew insisted I consider it. I still didn't want it, so to Lew's disappointment we dropped it from the list. A few weeks later I heard a Dylan song that I really liked and worked it up.

The next time I saw Lew, I said, "I found this great song," and played it for him. When I finished, he started laughing.

I asked him, "what's so funny?"

"Turley," Lew said with a smile, "I played that song for you three weeks ago. It was the Joan Baez version."

"Damn! That's the same song?"

"Sure is."

"Well, damn, let's record it. I guess producers are always right."

Lew and I had a great relationship that extended further than the workplace, and we're still friends today; we catch up with each other often.

Love Minus Zero was eventually chosen to be the single from the album that was simply titled, *Turley Richards*. The flip side was *Gone From Yesterday*. Promotional copies were sent out in November of 1969 for radio airplay. The single was issued for sale after the New Year, with plans for releasing the album soon afterward. Professionally, 1970 looked as if it would be a good year, and despite the reality of blindness finally closing in on me, in many ways it would.

We had worked hard on the album and thought that we had it nearly finished. At the end of the last recording session everyone had packed up and left the studio for the night except for Lew Merenstein, the recording engineer, and me. I walked through the empty studio to the control room and asked Lew and the engineer to set two mics up for me.

"I've worked this song up called *I Heard the Voice of Jesus* and I've got to do it." I looked at Lew, "I have to do it."

"No problem," Lew said, and they came out to the studio, got me set up, and then returned to the control room. I began to sing:

I heard the voice of Jesus say,
Come onto me and rest,
Lay down thy weary one, thy weary one lay down,
Lay thy head upon my breast . . .

The song is almost seven minutes long, and when I finished singing I sat for a moment, frozen. My body and spirit were both shaken. I put down my guitar and made my way to the control room door. Weak in the knees, I leaned against the doorframe and asked:

"What the hell just happened?"

"I don't know, man," Lew replied in a tearful voice. "At first I got cold chills, then I just started crying. I have never heard anything like that in my whole life."

I don't know why I chose that particular song, but eighteen months later, that seven minutes would be defined as the moment I began to believe.

When I left the studio, I didn't even consider that *The Voice of Jesus* would make it on the album. The original recording is just my guitar and me, but afterward Lew went to great lengths to give it a fuller, more epic feel. He added to my vocal a B3 organ, electric guitar, bass, and tambourine; then, toward the end, a string orchestra arranged by George Butcher. I was on tour at the time, and wasn't around for any of these additions, but when Lew sent me a cassette tape of his finished version I was blown away.

Al Kooper, the legendary keyboardist who recorded and toured with Bob Dylan and many others during the 1960s, was so moved by my vocal on *I Heard the Voice of Jesus* that he became an unofficial promoter of my recording, carrying a cassette with him to every radio station he visited. It was through Kooper's insistence that *I Heard the Voice of Jesus* got radio air play around the country, on FM stations that had the freedom to break from the conventional top forty play lists. Today, more than forty years later, I still get messages from people who say that when they heard or saw me perform *Voice of Jesus,* it somehow moved or changed them. In many ways, that's the highest compliment any artist could ask for. Recently, Al had this to say:

Speaking as a musician, Turley's version of *I Heard the Voice of Jesus* on Warner's is one of the greatest vocal performances I have ever heard in my life. The story goes that he performed it in the studio solo accompanying himself on acoustic guitar. Producer Lew Merenstein, taking a page from producer Tom Wilson's tactic book, overdubbed a whole orchestra over Turley's performance including a bravado arrangement string section. It *almost* covered that incredible vocal performance, but somehow that amazing voice cuts through. There are moments in his vocal when he sings four or five notes *at one time*! (Al Kooper, 2007)

The song certainly followed me while I was on tour throughout 1970. Sometimes when I performed *I Heard the Voice of Jesus,* some unusual and often funny things happened. In the summer of '70, I was part of the Schaefer Music Festival in Central Park. Held at the park's band shell, I was sandwiched in between Paul Butterfield's Blues Band and Jethro Tull. It was a rainy day, but the festival went on as planned, with a crowd that was just too big to turn away. I was told that before I began my set, the rain got a little heavier, with most of the crowd heading for cover wherever they could find it, but when I began *I Heard the Voice of Jesus,* the rain stopped, and the sun suddenly came out. According to those who were with me, the people who had run for cover slowly came back into the open to watch me and listen. I took the song to its climactic end and then, as I was told (because remember, I couldn't see it), the clouds came back, the rain came down, and everyone ran for cover again.

On another occasion, while performing at Fredonia College in New York, I had just started singing when the school's PA system overrode the sound in the auditorium.

I began singing, *"I heard the voice of Jesus say . . ."*

Then came another voice, "Billy Roberts, report to the Dean's Office. Billy Roberts to the Dean's Office."

I said, "Billy, if you're here, you better get yo' ass to the Dean's office."

CHAPTER 15

Throughout 1970 I toured with or opened for acts including the Moody Blues, the 5th Dimension, Poco, Steve Miller, Vanilla Fudge, Joni Mitchell, Richie Havens, Laura Nyro, Sarah Vaughn, and the hard rock band Spirit. It was at the Spirit concert in Belpre, Ohio, that I was close enough to home for my mom and dad, along with Uncle Hubert, were able to come and hear me sing. It was the first time my mom had ever seen me in concert. After my performance I asked her how she liked the show.

"Fine," she said, "but you didn't sing one single Platters song."

"Mom! It's my concert, it's not a Platters concert."

"But you sing *Twilight Time* better than the Platters!"

Knowing where my stubbornness came from, I decided to drop it; however, I got even with her at the next concert she attended.

During the show I told the audience, "I'd like to introduce my mom and family. They're over there—the woman with the blue dress on, who got mad at me at my last concert for not singing a Platters song. So here you go, Mom."

I started singing *Twilight* to the laughter of the crowd. This time back in the dressing room, mom had something else to say.

"Richard, you embarrassed me every inch of my life!"

"But did you like the song, Mom?"

"Yeah," and she giggled.

Although he had recently moved back home to California, when I asked Jake Butts if he would like to come on tour, he jumped at the offer, so Jake was with me for the Moody Blues tour. Jake told me that during my set, most of the other acts on the tour, such as Steve Miller, Poco, and the Moody Blues, would stand in the wings to watch and listen to me sing.

The Moody Blues were good guys, even though they kept to themselves and were in their own world. At one point in the tour, the flight to our next city was cancelled because of an air traffic controller strike. Instead of cancelling the show, the Moody Blues booked a private jet to get to Dallas/Ft. Worth. The tour was a wonderful experience with me playing arenas that sat fifteen to twenty thousand people, at least that's what Jake told me. Hell, I couldn't see them; we might as well have been in some neighborhood garage. Most important to me was the growing friendship between Jake and me.

At a show in San Francisco I was reminded of the pecking order of the performers in a humorous way. When acts are booked to play a venue, they sign a contract that includes a "rider clause." The clause explains the special requests the acts are making of the venue owners. Things like what drinks are to be in the dressing room, what kind of mustard is to be served at the buffet, or what type of piano has to be onstage. My rider was pretty simple: I was to be provided with a pot of coffee, two Ho-Ho's, and a stool.

When we played The Fillmore West in San Francisco the stage manager Clarence, was reading over the riders to make sure the Moody Blues and I got what we requested. He turned to the promoter and said:

"Hey, Bill! Is this Turley Richards big enough to be requesting a couple of Ho's?
"What?"

"It says here in his rider that we have to get him two Ho's."

Graham took the contract and read it. "No, man! He wants Ho-Ho's—those chocolate cakes."

Clarence looked at the rider again. "Oh shit, man!" and everyone there started laughing. "Just don't tell Turley about this," but of course the story was too funny not to make it back to me. Before I went on stage I heard Clarence's voice next to me, and I just couldn't resist!

"Hey Clarence," I asked him, "How big do I have to be for you to get me a couple of Ho's?"

Clarence broke out laughing. "Oh man, they promised me they wouldn't tell you about that!"

Never trust show people to keep a secret. To this day, I still have coffee and Ho-Ho's before I sing. I had a little scare when Hostess went out of business. I didn't know how I was going to perform without my Ho's (oops, Ho-Ho's). I was saved over the summer when they came back on the market.

There is a general idea that show people are so intent on rising to stardom that they step all over each other on their way to the top. Of course there are people like that in any line of work, but I think the generalization is unfair. Throughout my career, I've had good experiences and bad experiences with show people, but along the way, I had a few situations where fellow performers went out of their way to help me.

I had played Mister Kelley's in Chicago several times since the fall of '69, both as an opening act and as a headliner, but this time I was opening for the great jazz singer Sarah Vaughn. After the first night a review appeared in a local Chicago paper, where the music critic wrote that "the opening act was some singer that I can't remember much about, but he wore nice boots." Sarah Vaughn saw the review and was furious. The next night Vaughn knew the critic was in the audience and before she started, her show she spoke directly to him from the stage:

"Turley is a great singer, and I can't believe you would write something like that about him! The reason you can't remember him is because you were drunk, and the only reason you saw his boots is because that's all you could see while you were lying on the floor. So why don't you get your ass out of here right now!"

The crowd applauded as the critic got up and left the club.

I also went out on tour with Laura Nyro. Nyro was from the Bronx and had written many hits for artists like Peter, Paul, and Mary, Barbara Streisand, the 5th Dimension, Three Dog Night, and Blood, Sweat, and Tears. By 1970 Nyro had become a star herself with two hit albums.

People often told me that I was a very difficult act to follow. I sang with so much energy and intensity that I left the crowd exhausted. Shortly after I began opening for Laura Nyro, I got a phone call from Bob Schwaid saying I was being dropped from the rest of her tour.

"Why?" I asked, stunned.

"Nyro's management won't say," Bob answered, "but I'll bet it's because you're just too strong an opener and they don't like it."

"Is this what Laura Nyro thinks?"

"I don't know. I never spoke to her, just her management group."

After the show was over, I ran into Laura in the hall and she said, "Hey, Turley! I'll see you next Thursday."

I looked at her and said "I'm really confused."

"Why?"

"Your manager called my manager today, and said I was bumped off the tour."

"That's bullshit!" Laura cried and she grabbed my arm. "Come with me."

She found the nearest pay phone on the wall and called her manager, even though it was 11:30 at night. In between her sentences, I could hear her manager's voice on the line, but couldn't make out what he was saying.

"What's with this bullshit about Turley Richards being taken off the tour? That's not gonna happen . . . he stays on the tour . . . Oh, really? In that case, I won't finish the tour either!"

At this point the voice on the other line went up an octave.

"I mean it! Okay . . . okay." She turned to me, "Turley, you're back on the tour."

Laura hadn't hung up yet, and she asked me, "How much are you making?" I told her and she turned back to the phone. "I want him to be paid double what he's getting."

Yet another octave came from the phone. Laura hung up.

"It's done. Once again, Turley, I'll see you next Thursday," and with that she walked away.

I called after her, "Laura!"

She stopped and turned, "Yes?"

"Can you help me get me back to my driver?"

"Oh my God Turley! I'm sorry!" She came back, and I took her arm.

I did my first shows overseas in England, playing the Plumpton Jazz Festival with some very un-jazz-like acts including Black Sabbath and Deep Purple. In addition to the festival, I played a club called the Lyceum in London, with Klaus Voorman as my bassist. Voorman had been a member of Manfred Mann and a close friend of the Beatles. He even won a Grammy Award for designing one of their album covers. During rehearsals we took a break and Voorman came up to me to discuss how much I should pay him for the gig.

"I'm not really sure how much I'm supposed to pay you," I said.

"I'm not sure how much I should ask for," Voorman answered.

We talked about it a little until Voorman said, "Wait a minute, let me call Paul. He'll know what we should settle on," and then, as Laura Nyro had done, he got on the phone with me standing by. Voorman held the phone out so I could hear. The person he was calling picked up, "Hello."

"Hello Paul, this is Klaus. Listen, I'm standing here with Turley Richards from Warner Brothers. I'm playing a gig with him, and I wasn't sure what I should charge him."

"Who's paying for it?"

"Warner Brothers," I answered.

"If it's the record company," said Paul, "then charge them out the ass."

Klaus and I laughed, and Klaus said, "Good-bye, Paul."

"Was that Paul McCartney?" I asked.

"Yes."

"Oh my God," I said, laughing. "I hope Warner Brothers can afford it."

Before I played with Voorman or in the Plumpton Festival I was booked to open for Miriam Makeba at the Royal Albert Hall. Known as "Mama Africa," Makeba had scored a worldwide hit with her song *Pata Pata* in 1967. She was also managed and produced by team Schwaid-Merenstein.

The Royal Albert Hall was ninety-nine years old, and had seen some of the greatest performances in music history. Now I was playing there to a diverse British and European crowd who had come to see one of the biggest international singing stars of the time.

I was warming up in my dressing room, when there was a knock on my door and in came Mama Africa herself.

"Hello Turley," Makeba said, and then she introduced herself. I assumed that Bob Schwaid and Lew Merenstien had spoken to her about me. "I heard you singing as I was coming down the hallway just now," she continued. "You're an incredible singer, and such a beautiful voice!" I thanked her for her kindness. But she wasn't finished. She wanted to offer to do something during the show that absolutely blew me away.

"I want my audience to hear you, so I want to make sure that you have their attention. Instead of you opening, let me go on first. I'll sing two songs, and then I'll introduce you."

This was just unheard of—the headliner offering to introduce and then turn the audience over to the opening act. When it was show time Makeba came out first and began her show. At the end of her second song, she had maneuvered herself to stage left with the spotlight on her. As she spoke, I was directed to center stage, in the dark.

"Ladies and gentlemen, I'm going to stop for now because I want you to hear a man with one of the most beautiful voices I have ever heard. I first heard him backstage, and now I want you to hear him. I want you to listen to this man sing, and then I will return. Now everyone please welcome Mr. Turley Richards."

The spotlight and the crowd, then turned to me. Introduced by Makeba, I immediately had the audience's recognition, and after I began singing they were mine. Opening acts often struggle for the crowd's full attention, but through Makeba's selfless gesture, that wasn't a concern tonight. And the audience was rewarded with my best. Through the years I've said to myself that if I was ever in a position to do the same thing for another artist—something so empty of ego that it's nearly unheard of—that I would do it without hesitation.

Afterward I was invited by Makeba and her husband to an after-show party they were throwing. I was honored to be invited, and soon found myself at the party sitting with Makeba's husband, the American Civil Rights leader, Stokely Carmichael.

Carmichael was the leader of the Student Non-violent Coordinating Committee (SNCC) and later was the honorary prime minister of the Black Panthers. After talking about the show, we started talking politics and discovered we had some things in common. First, we were around the same age and grew up during the beginnings of the Civil Rights Movement. As we talked, we also discovered that both of us had been in Jackson in 1961 on the day of the Freedom Riders march. Small world, isn't it? That day my skin color gave me protection and a safe ride out of the city, but Carmichael's got him arrested and a prison sentence for entering a "whites only" cafeteria.

I could tell Carmichael was getting uncomfortable talking about his past, so I let him change the subject.

It had been a unique and great night.

CHAPTER 16

Warner Brothers released *Love Minus Zero* as a single in the winter of 1970 and it climbed to number fifty-four on the Billboard charts. They wanted to follow that with *I Heard the Voice of Jesus*, but my version played for almost seven minutes, which was too long for Top 40 AM radio stations to play in 1970. Even superstar acts, with the exception of the Beatles, had to edit songs to about three and a half minutes to get them on AM radio. Warner Brothers made several attempts to edit *Voice of Jesus*, but none of them worked. The way I sang the song lost its coherence and power without the whole performance, so *I Heard the Voice of Jesus* became a staple of my stage act, but was never released as a single.

For some unknown reason, the label didn't release the album until the fall of 1970, nearly a year after we finished recording, and at least six months since *Love Minus Zero* charted. It was virtually unheard of for a record label not to release an album right after the single charted. While I toured throughout 1970, I was promoting a single that had already charted, and an album that wasn't yet released. What made me angrier was Warner's lack of promotion. *Love Minus Zero* was a hit song, cracking Billboard's Hot 100. Nationally, the single made it to number fifty-four, but it did even better in major markets including San Francisco, Seattle, Houston, and Dallas, where it made the top ten play lists. There was a base to sell more records, but the label blew it, and by the time the album was released I was already at the tail end of my touring dates.

I always trusted Bob Schwaid, and felt that he had done right by me and my career, although there were mistakes. Bob had passed on the chance to perform at Woodstock, but who knew what Woodstock was going to turn into?

"It's just going to be a bunch of hippies," Bob had advised me, "and I can get you more money playing somewhere else."

I had agreed with Bob's judgment, and didn't hold that decision against him. This time, though, I found out from one of the agents at ICM, that Bob had passed up an opportunity that would have made me a household name. *The David Frost Show*, where I had already made five appearances, wanted me to come back for an entire year. He wanted me to appear Monday through Thursday night at eight in the evening, which was primetime. It would have been some two hundred shows where I would be featured, reaching a nightly audience of over fourteen million viewers. David wanted to share my positive attitude about how I was handling going blind with the viewers because he felt it would be inspirational to them. Managers—like attorneys—are required to bring all offers to their clients and advise them, but the ultimate decision always rests with the artist they represent. Bob Schwaid never even came to me with the offer.

"Why didn't you tell me about this?" I demanded from Schwaid.

"It was nothing, Turley. Besides, Carson wanted you back."

I exploded. "Let me get this straight! You turned down over two hundred appearances in primetime, with over fourteen million families for one night on Carson? I could have been a superstar! Are you out of your fucking mind! You just cost me a multimillion dollar career! And you never even presented it to me!"

Schwaid got within an inch of my face and yelled, "Goddammit! I'm managing your career, and you'll do what the fuck I tell you to do!"

He got too close. As a blind person, when someone becomes threatening, I react fast. I shoved him away from me pretty hard, and heard him fall. I said, "Fuck you, Bob. We're done." I walked out.

From that moment I was done with Bob Schwaid. To this day, when I think about it, my reaction is still total disbelief. My managers so far had been Schwartz, Shane, and Schwaid. I planned to stay away from anyone whose name began with an "S" or who had an office at 54th and 7th. I felt like a pawn in a chess game—no control over my future and sacrificed early in the game. Lew Merenstein was Bob's partner, and when I told Lew years later what Bob had done (or in this case had not done) he couldn't figure it out.

"Why would Bob turn that down?" Lew said in disbelief. I don't know Lew. I wish I did, but I don't.

I had a two album deal with Warner Brothers, and by the winter of '71, I was back in the studio recording my second album, *Expressions*. The album was recorded at the Record Plant in Los Angeles, this time with Paul Harris producing. My session musicians were James Taylor's band at the time, including Leland Sklar, Russ Kunkel, and Danny Kortchmar.

I wanted *Expressions* to have a different sound than the first album. I thought "Turley Richards" was too mellow, and aside from *I Heard the Voice of Jesus*, which sounded closer to the singer I was on stage, I felt the album fell short. *Expressions* would be different. The sound would be more varied, and my lyrics more personal.

I wrote seven of the ten songs, and along with my songs I did three covers. The cover songs were Gotham and King's *Child of Mine*, which later became one of my daughter, Amber's, favorite songs), Bob Dylan's It's *All Over Now Baby Blue*, and *My World is Empty* by Holland, Dozier, Holland.

Paul got everyone together, but allowed me to control the musical direction. It was the first time in my recording career when I felt like I had a band. It all sounded great, and the album was finished and ready to be released by the summer.

Expressions was completed when I was called into Warner Brother's New York headquarters on Madison Avenue. The label had a new marketing strategy to sell Turley Richards to the world. I always thought I was marketable because I was considered an outstanding performer who could sing any style of music, but now the label thought they had a great new angle for me.

When we arrived we were ushered into a conference room. Adrian whispered to me how the room was set up, with the pictures of three stars, Ray Charles, Stevie Wonder, and Jose Feliciano. Next to them was a picture of Turley Richards. I had a sick feeling in my stomach as the meeting began.

One of the promotion executives started, "What does Turley have over these other guys?"

I heard a female voice say, "Well, Turley is way better looking and he's sexy."

"Exactly," said the exec. "Sex appeal. The women love Turley in concert. They think he's sexy, and that's what we have, 'The Sexy Blind Singer!' "

I had made records throughout the sixties and had been a teen idol back home. I had lived and worked hard in New York to make it. I had been on *The Tonight Show*. I had been on the charts and had ended countless shows to standing ovations in every club and venue I played. By 1971 I was twenty-nine years old, and now I was going to be "The Sexy Blind Singer?" I shoved my chair back and stood up.

"Are you trying to sell records or get me laid? This is bullshit!" The room went dead. "The sexy blind singer? Fuck it! I'm out of here!" The meeting was over.

When we got outside I told Adrian what I wanted to do. "I want out! I want out of everything and everyone! Out of Warner Brothers, out of ICM, out from Bob Schwaid, and out of the recording business!"

"But what would you do?" Adrian was upset and suddenly a little scared.

"I'll manage. I can still work *Love Minus Zero* for several years. It's a hit record. People will want to book me."

It took about a week to see it all through. I stuck with my anger and resolve, and with a lawyer we found a loophole in my contracts that I could use to get out of each and every one. It was a clean break.

It's been said that success in the music business takes the right combination of talent and marketing. Talent can only take you so far. In retrospect, the people at Warner Brothers were only doing their job. I had a new album coming out and their assignment was to market me. I was a product that needed to be sold. The problem was, I just wasn't ready for the packaging they had in mind or the way they presented it to me. Blindness was my personal battle, and I certainly wasn't ready to commercialize it. I was so overwhelmed with trying to handle going blind. When all of the bullshit from managers, and record labels, and producers was piled on, my reaction was to retreat. I just wanted to leave it all behind.

CHAPTER 17

By 1971 my relationship with Adrian was in trouble. We had been together since 1969 when she showed up at my door wanting to stay for a few days, and never left. Adrian was someone I thought I could rely on. She seemed to understand what I was going through and wanted to be there for me.

By Christmas of 1969, I had taken the next step in our relationship, and we went to West Virginia to meet my parents. My mom liked her and was relieved that I had found someone who was going to be with me, and help me through my transition to blindness. What I didn't know was that Adrian wanted more. Adrian knew my mom was religious, and when we went to visit my parents, she played on my mother's faith. Adrian wasn't religious herself, but she knew which buttons to push.

"I want to be there for Turley," she kept telling my mom. "I love him and want to help him. But I don't want us to live together in sin. I want to get married."

They both started in on me about how good it would be and how great we'd be together—married that is. This went on for nearly the whole visit. Finally I couldn't take it anymore.

"Okay!" I said, "If the two of you'll get off my damn back, I'll marry you!" Nice proposal, but that was that. It was the first of many red flags in our relationship.

When we got married in February of 1970, my mom and dad made their first and only visit to New York City. My dad, who was still a country boy at heart, was impressed. "Look at the size of those buildings," he kept saying. "Look at all of these people and all of those cars."

Adrian continued her career, getting jobs as a model, while I started touring, and that's when another red flag went up. While I was away, Adrian would spend money—lots of money. She charged it all to our credit cards, and by the time I figured out what was going on, the tab was about $39,000. That's a lot of money today, but it was a small fortune back then. But Adrian would try to make it sound like she was saving us money. I called her one day from Manhattan, Kansas. Our conversation was the beginning of the end of her spending sprees.

"I just saved us $2,000 on a couch," she said.

"Um, how did you save us $2,000?"

"Well the couch really cost $4,500, but I got it for $2,500."

"$2,500 on a couch?!"

"We needed a nice couch."

"And thumb tacks? You charged thumb tacks?"

"I needed thumb tacks."

It was a pattern of behavior that would only grow worse during our short marriage. Adrian was aggressive and usually got what she wanted; she was also impulsive and manipulative. Today Adrian might have been given a formal diagnosis, and could have gotten the help she needed, but in 1970 getting help for mental health problems wasn't as acceptable as it is today. Her behavior was not easy to handle, and I had my own profound issues to deal with.

By the fall of '70 I had gone completely blind. My sight had hung on longer than Dr. Chandler had said it would—about a year and a half longer—but blindness had finally come, and it was final. I was always on edge, just on the verge of saying fuck it all. Some days if I could have, I would have gone off like a hermit, so dealing with Adrian and her problems just wasn't a good scenario, and certainly not what I had expected when I married her.

In the spring of '71 we made a decision to move out of New York City. I always tell people that New York City was the greatest city to go blind in because I could hold onto my independence to the very end (e.g., hailing garbage trucks). I had always loved the city, but when I broke ties with the recording industry, I felt that I needed to get out, at least for a while.

Through mutual friends, I was introduced to a married couple who were college professors about to take a year sabbatical in Europe. They needed someone to house sit in Interlaken, New Jersey, so the arrangement worked for us both. It turned out the husband was also a fan.

"I saw you open for Laura Nyro," he said when we met. "You were great, so I went out and bought your album."

"Oh, so you're the one!" I answered.

We hit it off, and so for $500 a month, which was the cost of maintenance, Adrian and I had a beautiful house on a lake. It was near the ocean with a Florida room, a swimming pool, a boat dock, and a boat. I wanted to take the boat out, but no one would let me drive; all in all it was a very sweet deal.

After we moved in, Adrian met a lot of our new neighbors. She became especially friendly with a family across the street. They were Pentecostals, who liked to have prayer meetings in their home, and they invited Adrian and me over for an evening.

"They're having a best-selling author over to talk to everyone," Adrian said. But I wasn't in the mood, and I especially didn't want to spend an evening with a bunch of "Holy Rollers."

"We have to go. I already said you would sing *I Heard the Voice of Jesus* for them."

"You did what?" I was really annoyed now. "Please don't tell anyone I'll sing for them before asking me." I agreed to do it just this once.

Adrian was right about the author who was invited to speak that evening. His name was Arthur Katz, and the year before he had published his first book, the bestselling *Ben Israel, the Odyssey of a Modern Jew*. Katz would go on to publish a dozen more books while founding his Arthur Katz Fellowship and Ministries. But on this quiet evening in Interlaken he gave us an intimate and powerful testimony to his beliefs. I was still somewhat uncomfortable with the religious fervor, but I listened to Katz and enjoyed his lecture.

I closed the get-together by singing *I Heard the Voice of Jesus*. Everyone loved it, and we all said our thank-yous and good nights. While we were talking with Arthur, Adrian said, "Turley, I invited Arthur to stay with us so he doesn't have to drive all the way back to New York tonight."

Once again, I wished Adrian had asked me first, and that bothered me, but I liked him so it was all right. When we got home, Adrian announced she had "things to do upstairs" and left me alone with Arthur in the Florida room. I later found out that the entire evening had been manipulated by Adrian and the neighbors in order to convert me to Christianity. Adrian had convinced them that she was a Christian. At the time, though, all I knew was that I was left alone to talk with Arthur.

Initially, Katz was full of praise. "You know, Turley," he said, "your singing is simply amazing. It's a God-given gift. I've never heard anyone sing like you before. I believe with your singing voice you've been chosen by God."

I wasn't interested, and really just wanted to go to bed. Naturally the conversation turned to God and religion with Katz as minister, and me playing the doubting Thomas role.

Around 3 AM, after listening to my resistance for three hours, Katz said the words that would change me spiritually.

"Turley, you seem to think that Jesus will only come to you with a red carpet and trumpets blaring, with you on one end and Jesus on the other, and with both of you running toward each other in slow motion with arms outstretched."

I had told Katz about the night I recorded *I Heard the Voice of Jesus* and sat stunned afterward. Now he used that story to drive his point home. Katz said, "The night you sang *I heard the Voice of Jesus* in the recording studio is the night I believe you were saved. He entered your life that night, and the lives of the others who were in the control room. That's why you found them overwhelmed and crying."

Until that moment, despite my mom's spirituality, I had never realized the importance of God. I had spoken to God before in times of need, such as the night I almost committed suicide, but even that was tongue in cheek (remember God's bookie)? However, I did have to recognize the profound spiritual experience that happened that night in the studio, as well as the subsequent times I had performed the song. Now Arthur Katz had me thinking about it and connecting the dots of all those experiences and realizing that they related to God.

Together, Arthur and I held hands and he prayed as I accepted Jesus as my Savior. When we were finished, I had an idea and said to Arthur, "I feel pretty good! Why don't I go wake up Adrian, and have her accept Jesus Christ too?" Arthur laughed, and I think he got the point.

At the time, Arthur Katz had already made several appearances on Kathryn Kuhlman's *I Believe in Miracles* television show. Kuhlman was a faith healer, and although I wasn't sure I believed in such things, I was at least open to the possibility after my evening with Katz. Later that year, Kuhlman made an appearance in Pittsburgh, and when we heard about it Adrian and I decided to go.

It was during the prayer portion of Kuhlman's appearance that she instructed the audience to ask God for something personal. I naturally asked God to give me sight. I wasn't testing God, and this wasn't an "Okay, prove to me you're real" experiment. My prayer and request were sincere: "Please God, give me sight."

A month passed, and of course my eyesight didn't return. However, as time passed, I began to realize that God had answered my prayer. I had gained sight, but it was insight not eyesight. I was now able to better understand my personal situation and how my past behavior had played a part in my current position. This gave me insight into how I had to go forward with my life. I realized how foolish I had been during the spring, walking away from contracts with the biggest labels in music and the biggest talent agency in the world. I was offended and insulted by Warner Brothers angle of "The Sexy Blind Singer," but instead of talking about it and letting them know why I didn't like it, and working with them to find alternatives, I had stormed out and gotten a lawyer. It was just show business being show business, and I was being ignorant.

More vitally important, I re-discovered what my mom had always taught me throughout my childhood that defeat was no option. I had certainly reached a point in my life where I needed to remember that. I was blind, with an uncertain professional future, and in a difficult marriage. If my voice was indeed "God-given," as Arthur Katz claimed, then I needed be true to myself, and to honor God and my mother for the strength and confidence she had always given me. The only way out was by moving forward.

That night in Interlaken, I became a Christian. When people ask me, I usually tell them I'm a "Christian with an edge." I think that like a lot of people, I've tried to accept Christ's teachings in a personal way, without wanting to preach or impose my beliefs on others. I also like to choose what I believe are Christ's most important teachings, and to live by them the best way I can. To me, God and His son are not about punishment or retribution, but rather, about mercy, compassion, and forgiveness. The reason my mom loved to read and quote the Bible, was because she understood what life needed to be about.

With insight, I was now ready to go forward.

"Turley at the EXPLO '72 in Dallas with the Reverend, Billy Graham and Bill Bright. While performing at the EXPLO, I shared the stage with Johnny Cash, Kris Kristofferson, and Connie Smith."

CHAPTER 18

By the end of 1971 I needed a change of scenery. This had been the longest time in seven years that I was without a record label or a manager. From the notoriety of *Love Minus Zero*, I was still able to make a living performing in those regions where it was most successful. On both a personal and professional level though, I needed a break. I also needed to put some space between myself and Adrian, whose behavior was becoming more and more erratic.

The place I chose for my "sabbatical" was Louisville, Kentucky, a city with which I was already familiar. My friends Mickey and Sandy were from Louisville, and I had stayed with Mickey's family when the Gene Pitney tour played Louisville. That was back in 1966, and Mickey was playing at a club called The Shack, which was owned by Eddie Donaldson. I sat in with Mickey and the owner loved my singing, and asked me if I would like to return for a couple of nights. I told him I was on tour with Gene Pitney and was unavailable; Eddie told me to call him when I was available. I had heard that one of my jazz idols, the great trumpet player Clark Terry, was performing the next night, and asked Eddie if that was true. He said it was, and I told Eddie I wanted to come back on the chance that I might be able to sit in again.

"I guarantee you will." Eddie said.

I did return the next night, and it was a great thrill to perform a couple of songs with Clark Terry.

I took Donaldson up on his offer the following year, returning for a week to play at his new club "18 Washington Street." Now, almost five years later, I called Eddie Donaldson again. Donaldson was excited and told me he had caught me on the *Tonight Show*.

"How soon can you get down here?" was his reply. He booked me four weeks at his newest club, The Red Dog Saloon, and offered me a place to stay in his home. In January of 1972 I headed down to the city that soon would become my home.

Louisville sits on the Ohio River and is famous for being the home of the Kentucky Derby. Louisville is known for supporting the arts, with a strong music scene that I felt I could fit into. Since Adrian wasn't making this trip I needed someone who could get me around, so I hired Kenny Meyers. I had met Kenny while playing some gigs in Asbury Park, and when I asked him if he could come with me to Louisville, he was eager to jump on board. I guess Kenny needed to get away from home as much as I did. So, after the New Year, we loaded up and headed for Kentucky, with Kenny as my "roadie" and driver.

I played Eddie Donaldson's club for four weeks, and it was a good run. Rod Burbridge, who worked for the television station WHAS in Louisville selling commercial time, came in several times to hear me sing. One evening he introduced himself.

"Man, you're great. Have you ever thought about doing a pilot?"

"It depends on what she looks like!" I said.

Rod laughed. "No man, a television pilot. I think you would be great having a musical television show."

"I never thought about it, but it sounds like a great idea," I said. "What do we need to do?"

I asked Rod if we could shoot it there, in the club, but he said that no, it had to be done in the station. I strongly felt I needed a live audience, so I asked Rod to give me a couple of days to get some people together who would come to the studio.

Rod arranged for me to shoot the pilot at the WHAS studios. It was short—about twenty-five minutes—which would be about the length of the actual television show. For the pilot I would talk and sing as if I were on stage. No problem with that. We shot the pilot, and I had a good time with the audience. The television crew and Rod Burbridge were happy, so now all I needed were some sponsors for the show and we'd be in business.

"Okay, Rod," I said, "when do I find out if we've got a show? I'm leaving for New Jersey in a few days."

"Don't worry, man. As soon as I find out I'll call you."

I drove back to New Jersey with Kenny, stopping along the way in West Virginia to visit my mom and dad and to think about the possibilities ahead of me. The trip had turned out better than I could have hoped. Now I just had to wait for Rod to call with the good news. Back in Interlaken I waited . . . and waited . . . and then waited some more. A week and a half went by, but no call from Rod. Finally the phone rang.

"The station loved the pilot, Turley, but we can't find any sponsors. I tried everybody, but I'm striking out. I'm sorry man, but no sponsors, no show."

I thought fast. No way could I let an opportunity like this slip by. "Just give me a couple of days," I told Rod, "I'll find somebody."

I called some people I had met back in Louisville, and through mutual friends I was put in contact with Newell Fox, a wealthy businessman who owned nine Burger King Restaurants in and around Kentucky. I flew back to Louisville to meet with Fox and show him the pilot. Fox liked what he saw and, after some discussion, agreed to back what became *The Turley Richards Show*—a half-hour, summer telecast showcasing local Louisville talent and me. We would begin production in June.

I was making a good living playing clubs and colleges, and even began playing for the artsy avant-garde crowd. Even some locals who were into the drug culture started digging me, after hearing me at Bellarmine College where I performed a song that spoke their language. Someone later told me that after the concert, they saw graffiti on campus that read: *Who needs Dylan, we have Turley.* Hey, some people get their name in lights—I get mine in graffiti.

I've never been the type of songwriter who can write with purpose. A song comes out of me, and sometimes months go by before I realize what it's about. In the latter part of 1971, I wrote two songs, *Ugly Trip* and *Pain*. Once I started performing them, I realized that each time a little bit of the pain and personal demons haunting me dissipated. One of the venues where I performed both songs was a concert at Bellarmine College in 1972 that we recorded as a live album.

The Bellarmine show was set up so that when people entered, they were given a stub that was redeemable later for the album. After the show, I put in the order for nearly a thousand albums, and when they came in, the customers came back to the college to pick them up. It was a good promotional idea, a big success, and one of the greatest live performances of my career.

A week later, I sat down with artist Marilyn Green to develop an album cover. In the process of explaining to her what I wanted, the title came to me clear as a bell: *From Darkness to Light.* I've often said that I had to go blind to see, meaning looking beyond physical appearances to "see" what a person is really like.

Through the Bellarmine show, I gained some new fans and good friends, including Bob Tiell. After the concert, Bob told me he had tagged along with his girlfriend to the show, and was blown away by my "crazy singing voice." He asked me if I wrote all of my songs, and when I told him that I did, he said he was really affected by the lyrics, that they were "extremely heavy."

We stood and talked for a few minutes, and I told him that if he got the chance, he could come to the television studio where we would be taping the show in June, and sit in as part of the studio audience. I told him the first show was taping on my birthday, and he commented that his was a couple of weeks earlier. Bob did show up at the studio, and he remembered it was my birthday.

Before the show started, Bob came to my dressing room. He told me he had to leave town right after the show, so he wanted to give me a little something before he left. As I took it from him, someone in the dressing room told me it was a cupcake with a candle in it.

"Happy birthday," Bob said.

"Wow. Cupcake? Candle? You are straight, aren't you, Bob?"

Everyone in the room laughed, including Bob.

When Bob came to my apartment for the first time, we discovered a shared passion that was to become a cornerstone of our friendship.

Seeing my Boston Celtics mug on top of the television, Bob asked, "are you a Celtics fan too?"

"Hell yeah," I said. "Bill Russell is da man!"

You can't be a Celtics and Bill Russell fan and not be friends.

Bob has tremendous intelligence that he puts to good use. Bob was also great fun. We hung out together, constantly trying to outdo each other in contests of sports trivia. Today we still meet regularly to have breakfast and trade trivia questions. Bob will admit, I am hard to stump in trivia, but he never stops trying. I can say the same for him.

While hosting *The Turley Richards Show*, I reached out to the media to seek additional promotion through radio and newspaper interviews. Along the way, I met another lifelong friend, Paul Steinmetz, who when interviewed for this book, had this to say:

"I first met Turley when I interviewed him for a music paper called 'The Licorice Frisbee,' I had done some freelance writing for *Rolling Stone* and *Crawdaddy,* and had some bad experiences interviewing musicians who were usually self-absorbed with big egos. A lot of them led isolated and sheltered lives where everything was mapped and planned for them, and most weren't interested if you had a deadline to meet. But meeting Turley was a completely different experience. When I went to his apartment for the interview, I met someone who was friendly and gracious. He even offered me a cup of coffee. This just never happened. Talking to him I realized that this was a man who was concerned about more than just himself.

"We hit it off and found out we liked a lot of the same music, including being big fans of Ray Charles. And that's when we got into a friendly argument about what type of music Ray Charles played. Was he R&B or jazz or the blues? I said that Charles was jazz, but Turley wouldn't agree.

"When I needed to go, Turley thanked me and asked for my phone number so we could continue our conversation; again, something that never happens. Then late that night my phone rings and it's Turley wanting to apologize for our friendly argument about Ray Charles. 'Oh, and by the way,' Turley said before he hung up, 'Ray Charles is not jazz.' We became good friends after that."

Paul Steinmetz is an intellectual man with a love for writing and music. He had written some good words about my television show, and so when he asked me for an interview I was happy to oblige.

After the interview, Paul became a fan and showed up at my gigs around Louisville. Eventually we became good friends, who called each other often even after Paul moved out of state to follow his writing career. I like to talk with someone as intelligent and opinionated as Paul, and we looked forward to our friendly arguments. It was always fun to disagree with Paul, but there was one disagreement Paul couldn't win with me. "Turley," he would say, "you need to go more commercial with your music."

"Paul," I would answer wearily, "six record labels tried that in the sixties, and it didn't work then. Why would it work now?" End of argument.

The show became a hit, and WHAS and Newell Fox couldn't have been happier with the ratings I brought in. In television, ratings equal revenue and profits, and *The Turley Richards Show* was a winner. Through the show I became a local celebrity and, as the host and co-producer, I was the first blind person in television history to star in and produce their own weekly television show.

As co-producer, I worked with the station's regular producer Harris Rodgers and helped arrange the format, which was part talk and part entertainment. I composed a song for the intro to the show, and performed it before introducing the musical artists for the evening. The audience was arranged close to the action on two sides of the studio, and in the middle I would interview my guests before they performed.

We shot thirteen episodes in three weeks, the first being on my birthday in June. The first broadcast was in the beginning of July. WHAS scheduled us for 8:30 on Thursday evenings—a prime viewing night—throughout the summer. I turned out to be a good interviewer, and I was proud of the production quality of the show, even on my voice-overs when I would advertise that week's coming episode.

Of course, no television show is shot without some bloopers, and mine was no exception, but since I never do anything halfway, mine was the blooper of all bloopers. We shot the show in segments that, when aired, were separated by the sponsor's commercials for Burger King whose catchphrase was "It takes two hands to handle a Whopper."™ At the end of the segment one day, I decided to ad lib and throw in a line for the sponsor using their catchphrase. As usual, I was right on target with my timing, but unfortunately what came out of my mouth was "Hey, we'll be right back after this commercial, and don't forget—it takes two hands to handle my whopper"!

The co-producer screamed, *"Cut!!"* in a horrified voice and ran over to me.

"What's wrong?" I asked.

With teeth clenched he whispered, "Turley, do you realize what you just said?"

I didn't, and when told me, I was shocked and embarrassed (and I don't embarrass easily). I had heard the laughter from the audience and later, after some time had passed, I thought it was funny too. On that day, though, there were kids in the audience, and it was not funny. We had to re-shoot the entire segment, which meant my guest had to sing again. I apologized to the audience. There would be no more ad libs in my future. Maybe.

As the show's host and co-producer who had the backing of the sponsor, I had the final say on who would appear each week. As I was reviewing the weekly line-ups with the station managers, we came to the Ramon Howard Band, a dynamite jazz and R&B group from the west end of Louisville.

"Well, we can't have them on," the station programmer said. "I've seen them and they're all black."

I could tell right away what I was dealing with, so with heavy sarcasm I replied, "No, their trumpet player is white."

"Yeah, well, I mean—"

"Listen," I said, "let me ask you something. This is 1972, not '52, so what the hell are you saying?"

"We just don't usually have blacks on, we just can't—"

"Now wait," I interrupted again, "You're saying you don't want black people on, but Faith Lyles is on the omelet show in the morning with Milton Metz, and for god's sake, one of my camera guys is black"!

He turned to the station manager and said, "It'll hurt our numbers."

Now I was pissed.

"You're a racist," I said.

The program director slammed his fist down on the table. He went into a macho tough-guy rant about how he knew what he was talking about and how I needed to listen to him.

"You don't want to be getting macho with me," I said.

The station's general manager jumped in.

"No-no guys, hold on. That's enough." He turned to the program director. "Listen, Turley has a right to have whoever he wants to have. He has the sponsor."

The program director stormed out. We had the Ramon Howard Band on the show, and the station didn't get any backlash about having black artists on during prime time.

As the show's season progressed, the bigger problem we ran into was money. Having local talent on was fine (Mickey Clark had been one of my guests), but as good as Mickey and the Ramon Howard Band were, I wanted to break out of Louisville and include nationally known stars. In particular, I wanted the type of artists I had met during my career, such as folk singer Odetta, and my friend Richie Havens. The station wanted that too, but not bad enough to kick in the extra money needed to attract star names. Newell Fox also had a fixed budget, so when WHAS asked me to sign a five-year extension for the show, to their surprise I turned them down.

"There's just no way," I told them, "that I can keep the show a hit while relying on local talent only. It just won't last. We have to attract bigger names." But the station wouldn't budge, and that was that.

Was I foolish turning down a five-year contract? Maybe. The show was a hit, and with *The Turley Richards Show* I was given the most creative control I had ever enjoyed in my career, and I made it work. I honestly believed it wouldn't hold its success using only local talent and I didn't want to be remembered as the host of a failing television show, so I thought it was best to get out while I was on top.

CHAPTER 19

While I was visiting my parents in St. Albans, West Virginia, we had a family get-together.

Aunt Flossie had been in the backyard the day I was hit by the arrow. She was the fun Aunt we all liked to tease, and she would play along pretending to be offended, while (I was told) a half smile played on her face.

At the get-together she came over to sit with Lonnie and me.

"Oh Richard," she said, "you know if I could I'd give you one of my eyes."

"Now Flossie, what would I want with one of your beady little eyes?"

"Well, you can just kiss my ass!"

"You wouldn't want those eyes anyway, Richard," said Lonnie, "they go to sleep by nine o'clock."

"You can just kiss my ass too!" She got up and started to walk away, stopped and half turned back to us. "As a matter of fact, all of ya can kiss my ass!" We roared with laughter.

I knew that Aunt Flossie's offer came from the heart—about giving me one of her eyes, that is. I truly loved Flossie, and I miss her.

When I went fully blind in 1970, I knew I would have to rely on others more than ever. Doing this would require some concentrated effort because my goal was to stay independent and to need others as little as possible. I was fortunate I had friends and family I knew I could count on. Moving back to West Virginia was the last thing I planned to do, but it was still good to know that people were there I could always turn to. Flossie couldn't give me an eye, but I knew that she'd be willing to become my eyes if I needed her.

The one person I was willing to accept help from was my wife, Adrian, and she did see me through my transition to blindness. Adrian had serious issues of her own that she needed to address—very serious issues that I wasn't in a position to handle. Adrian had a friendly personality that people took to immediately, but in retrospect it was all a cover. Unfortunately, behind the open and friendly personality was a sad and insecure person who used manipulation to build herself up.

When we first met she seemed to be understanding and helpful, and I felt lucky to have her. Today I realize that what on the surface seemed to be helpfulness was really enabling. It kept me dependent on her for help. Maybe she didn't do it consciously, but the result was a bitter and destructive relationship.

Adrian nearly bankrupted us with the $39,000 spending spree she'd had while I was on tour, and because of that, I had to do a sort of "chargecardectomy" on her. Much to her chagrin, she was only allowed to have credit cards with a $200 limit. You would have thought I had cut off one of her legs. So, it shouldn't have been a big surprise shortly after when my brother Fred told me she had called him and asked for a $15,000 loan. To make matters worse, she asked Fred not to tell me about it. Fred said he would be happy to help, but not if it was behind my back. She wouldn't say what she needed the money for and the conversation ended. I really knew the marriage was headed for disaster when she called my mother and said that I was physically abusing her. My mom, almost in shock, started to believe her until Adrian took her story a step too far.

"He beats Kion too," Adrian went on. "He kicks him and throws him against the wall."

"Well," Mom said with relief, "you almost had me believing you until you said Richard beats Kion, and there's no way Richard would hurt that dog. He loves him too much, and he would rather die. Besides, the dog is 110 pounds, so I don't think he would let anybody beat him."

The pattern repeated with lying, manic spending, trying to borrow money, and constant erratic behavior. I asked Adrian over and over again why she did these things, and, "I don't know," was her only answer. Then I would tell her she had to get help, to which she would reply that she didn't need it.

She did admit that our marriage was in trouble, so I asked her if she was willing to go to marriage counseling, and she agreed to go. After meeting with the counselor, he put us in a group. The counseling group turned out to be a joke, with one woman claiming that a spot on her kitchen wall was the Devil watching her, while four other women were there without their husbands. I remember asking the group leader what any of this had to do with marriage, and all he said was that it would all work out in time. At that point, Adrian and I got up and left. Our marriage was unraveling, and I was at my wits end.

As a last resort, I called Adrian's mother hoping she could shed some light on her behavior, but all she could tell me was that Adrian had been doing these things since high school. I wanted to help her, but, again, how do you help someone who doesn't want it?

Adrian moved to Louisville with me in June when I began taping the television show, but by the end of the year we were separated, and by February of '73 we had signed divorce papers. Considering how I proposed to her, our marriage probably ended better than it began.

From the strength of the television show, I was well-known regionally, and finding singing gigs, at clubs, colleges, or private parties, was never a problem. I needed help getting around town, but fortunately I had plenty of friends and fans who always wanted to lend a hand. Cleaning house became an issue, but I could always hire someone to do that. I knew I could earn a good living—it was living that became the problem.

This wasn't the first time I was on my own, but with Adrian gone it was the first time I was on my own and blind. I wasn't homeless as I had been in Central Park, but I had that same alone feeling. I still didn't go to rehab. I was so stubborn and so intent on not being the "typical" blind person that I was adamant—I was going to figure everything out by myself. Everyday things that most people take for granted, like driving to an appointment or cooking dinner, became obstacles I had to address.

Cooking on a stove was a problem, and microwaves weren't common then. I relied on take-out, but if I really needed to cook, I had to use the oven. Frozen pot pies and chicken tenders became Chef Turley's oven-roasted specialties. The oven was a problem too, because it was gas, and I had to light it. Reaching in with a match wasn't easy, but I always had Kion sticking his snout in to supervise. When I started using eighteen-inch matches, the job got easier. I would feel with one hand for the hole where the gas came out, and then put the match over it.

One time though, after turning on the gas I had some trouble maneuvering with the match and too much gas came out before I reached the hole. *WHOOOOOSH!* The flame shot out. Kion turned tail and ran out the kitchen door. I went to him to see if he was okay, and when I touched him, I found that he was looking around the door, staring at the oven to see what had happened. I could smell the burned hair, and when I felt his face I discovered his eyebrows were singed. After that, whenever he saw me open the oven door, Kion would hightail it to his safety spot halfway around the kitchen door. I have to admit, I sometimes used him as a kind of parlor trick when friends visited. I would call him into the kitchen only to open the oven door and have them watch him run for cover and then peek his head around the corner while everyone laughed.

By 1973 I was no longer the naïve kid trying to make it in music. I was a show biz veteran who saw the music business for what it was—a business. So, when I wanted to get back to playing soul, R&B, and rock, I put together a hot band of the best local talent I could find. On keyboards I had Dan Hurley, a great jazz player who eventually became a music professor. On drums was Randy Erhlich; on bass Tom Johnson; and on guitar, Chuck Smith who was a singer/songwriter from a local band called Babe Ruth.

The band was hot, but unfortunately for the other guys I quickly found out that I could make a lot more money playing solo, so we eventually disbanded. I remembered what good musicians the guys were, and when I got the chance to make a new album I gave each of them a call.

It was fall of 1973 and two and a half years since I'd had a recording contract or had made a studio record, but now an opportunity came from a fledgling label called Calliope Records. I got a call in September from owners Ron Willins and Lee Weisle asking if I'd like to record for them. Ron and Lee flew me out to LA where we talked and worked out a contract. In March of 1974, I was back with my Louisville band to record in the Wally Heider Studios in Hollywood. It was another new album and another new start. I was savvy enough by now to expect some problems, so the minor disagreements that came up weren't a big deal. The deal-breaker was an argument over what to title the album.

"We're going to call it 'The Prince of Darkness,'" Lee said.

"The what?" I asked.

"The Prince of Darkness. It's because you're blind, get it?"

"Lee, do you know who the Prince of Darkness is? It's Satan!"

"Well, so what?"

"Lee, I'm a Christian. I can't put out an album with that title."

"Who cares? It's a great title."

"I care."

The story doesn't end there. I had to retain an attorney, who was referred to me by a friend of Jake Butts. Eventually everything was settled, and everyone was satisfied, but there was no record released.

It was back to Louisville to start again.

After I got back from Los Angeles, I played a charity show at Eastern High School in Louisville. A girl named Cindy Flannigan had arranged the event.

Afterward she started helping me out by shopping for my groceries. In late May, on one of these shopping days, Cindy showed up at my house to get my grocery list, and brought a friend. She introduced her friend as Patty Kirchner, and told me she had brought her along because Patty wanted to meet me.

The two girls were in the kitchen making a grocery list, when things got real quiet. A minute later, Cindy came into the other room.

"Okay, Turley," Cindy said, "I'm going to the store now. Be right back." And she was gone

"So," I said to Patty, "what did you do, write a note to Cindy telling her to go shopping and leave you here?"

Patty was shocked. "Oh god, you heard me write that to her?"

There was instant chemistry between us, and we dated for nearly a year before Patty moved in with me. Patty was the polar opposite of Adrian. She could be very shy when meeting new people. Some mistook this and thought she was standoffish until they got to know her. Once Patty got to know people, they realized how sweet and funny she was. With Patty I was in a relationship with someone I knew I could trust and count on.

I hadn't had a recording contract in five years, but if I was going to make a life with Patty, and maybe start a family, then I needed to break out professionally.

With the Calliope fiasco behind me, an opportunity arose to try television again. Through a contact I met from Ohio, I was asked to be involved in a syndicated television show with William Stanley (not his real name), a television producer.

When I met with William, I asked him to outline the format for the show. The show would be called *The Wonderful World of Music,* and filming would be in Hollywood where I would co-host the show each week with a well-known celebrity. William said he believed he could get the show sold into syndication, but the funds had not been raised yet. I told him I had experience raising money for my previous show, and asked him to give me a shot at it for this show. I knew that it was easy to raise funds using venture capital because of the huge write-offs. I asked William to give me his resume so that I would have something to present to potential investors.

I remembered a millionaire I had met who lived in Boca Raton, Florida, and I gave him a call and explained my situation. He was interested and told me he would put together an investment party. Two weeks later, he called me back with a date and asked me if I could make it. I called William to see if he could meet me there. He told me he would be out of the country, but he trusted me to handle the party on my own.

There were twenty-two investors who attended the party in Boca Raton where I performed and did a presentation that explained the show's format. The investors were impressed to the tune of one million dollars (my kind of tune)! We agreed that the money would be deposited to an account in Los Angeles and that William and I would be the sole signatories on the account. I wish I had insisted on a double signature requirement.

Within a week in Los Angeles, we had shot the pilot and two additional shows, which was one more than we had contracted for. My guest for the pilot was the great singer Johnny Mathis, who had a dozen gold and platinum records. It was a half-hour show that included both my guest and me performing along with a segment where I interviewed the guest. It was a fabulous show and a great thrill for me because Johnny was one of my all-time favorite singers. He was also on the San Francisco Dons track team with my hero, Bill Russell, which made me even more anxious to meet him.

For the second episode, my guest was Grammy-winning country singer Lynn Anderson of *I Never Promised You a Rose Garden* fame. The taping went without a hitch. The third episode, purely by accident became the most memorable.

We were working in the studio when someone mentioned that the comedian Jonathan Winters was taping a show down the hall.

"Jonathan Winters?" I asked. "I'd love to meet him; he's one of my all-time favorite comedians."

Someone must have told him because as we were working I suddenly felt a hand on my shoulder.

Someone said, "Turley?"

"Yeah," I answered.

"Jonathan Winters."

I could kick myself today for not asking others to take pictures of me and all of the famous people I've worked with, but this time someone was ready, and they caught the moment when I realized it was Jonathan Winters greeting me. I've been told the expression on my face is like a little boy who is being given a game ball by his hero. We talked and joked for a while.

I told Winters that I wished I could see him, since a lot of his comedy was visual, to which he replied, "Well, then I must be good, if I can make you laugh."

"Oh, by the way," I said, "I used to be managed by Norman Schwartz."

"Oh my God, I love Norman!" Winters exclaimed.

I told him we were taping a pilot and asked if he could do a bit for the show. "I'd love to," he said, and so he became my guest for the third episode.

With the three episodes done, I left post-production to William Stanley, and flew back to Louisville. A few days later, I called him to check on how things were going, but there was no answer. Over the next couple of weeks I kept trying every few days, but he never answered the phone, and never returned my messages. At this point, I was pissed off that he wasn't calling me back, but I also felt suspicious that something might not be kosher.

I wasn't sure what to do next, so I started with the bank, and called them to find out what the current balance was. After I gave them all of my identifying credentials, the teller read me the balance. There was one dollar in the account. One dollar!? I was dumbfounded, and then the teller told me that over the last ten days there had been three separate withdrawals of $300,000 each. I hung up the phone. All I could think of was the Florida investors and how screwed I was. It was one of a very few times in my life when I felt genuine fear. Regardless, I called them pretty quickly (about ten minutes later) and gave the bad news to my friend. He took it fairly well, all things considered, and assured me that none of the investors would suspect I had anything to do with it. He also assured me that they would find William Stanley. I hoped I would hear back from my friend, or that William Stanley would surface. Neither William Stanley nor the episodes were ever seen again.

"The photo of that magic moment that I shared with Jonathan Winters."

CHAPTER 20

There was one unfinished personal issue that I needed to address, and it was Patty who saw me through this.

"Your right eye has nearly ruptured," I was told by Dr. Rachit, who had taken over for Dr. Chandler when he retired.

"What do I need to do?" I asked him.

"I think it's time to have your eye removed. Your glaucoma has finally damaged it to the point where it is hemorrhaging and there is no reason to keep it any longer. Also, if we remove the eye you won't have to take your medication anymore."

I readily agreed to the surgery. I had always wanted this, but the doctors insisted I should wait in case science developed a way to repair my vision. They stressed the point that this would be impossible if I didn't have an eye to work with, so I continued taking the medication. Now the choice was taken away, and I felt relieved. I wouldn't have to take my glaucoma meds anymore, which for eight years wreaked havoc with my health, causing dehydration, pain, and weight loss.

We went back to Charleston for the surgery. My mom sat in the waiting room with Patty.

"It kills me to see him hurt," Patty said. "He's my superman."

Everything went well, and without those horrible meds my health and quality of life improved. About a month later, I had two prosthetic hand-painted eyes that made my mom cry the first time she saw them. She said they looked just like my eyes did when I was four.

With the television show a bust, I decided to take another shot at recording. Patty and I were making a life together and I needed to build my income. To get a new recording contract I did something that I tell new artists never to do—make a demo and send it to multiple record companies. Without a connection or introduction these demos almost never get heard, but I went against my own advice and took a shot, as though I were an up-and-coming new artist trying to make it. I made the decision with the belief that I would be taken more seriously because of my hit record with Warner Brothers (*Love Minus Zero*). I made a demo tape of four songs, sent them out to ten record labels, and to my surprise I got back nine responses with offers of a contract.

I thought through the offers, and then chose the one from CBS/Epic Records. Epic was based in Nashville, which is pretty close to Louisville, and I chose them out of convenience. Close to home meant Patty and I wouldn't need to uproot ourselves. When I signed with Epic they became my seventh record label. Maybe seven would be my lucky number.

In late '76 I came home from signing the Epic contract, and found Patty in the kitchen. I immediately sensed that she was nervous.

"Is something wrong?" I asked her.

"Well, um . . . I went to the doctor today."

"The doctor? Are you okay?"

"Well, um, well . . . I'm going to have a baby."

"That's incredible!" was my instant reaction. I went and hugged her.

"I was so scared you'd be mad."

"No, it's great, honey!" I felt Patty's tension melt away. "We have to get married," I said, and so the next day we went to the Justice of the Peace. I was a husband again and soon to be a father.

West Virginia Superstar would be my fourth album. It was cut in Nashville at Quadrophonic Studios, and Troy Sills and Epic's Vice President Ron Bledsoe became my producers. My studio musicians were Kenny Malone, a great drummer and bass players, Jessie Boyce and Norbert Putnam. Norbert was also one of the owners of the studio. The co-owner, David Briggs, who played keyboards, had also toured with Elvis for many years; Shane Keister, who would be the first keyboardist in Nashville to use "programming" in his work; and Reggie Young and Teddy Irwin on guitars. Teddy had recorded with Neil Young and Johnny Cash, and had played for me on *I Heard the Voice of Jesus*. Engineering the album would be the legendary Gene Eichelberger. This album was the beginning of a long friendship with Gene.

One of the tracks was also the title of the album. The song was written as a sort of self-portrait, and covered the years since I had left West Virginia. We recorded the album live in the studio, just the musicians and me playing each song as if we were in front of an audience. Everything jelled. The players were hot, and my voice was dead on and powerful. The studio guys loved it, and we all felt it was a great record.

I had to go out on the road for some shows, and when I came back I was horrified to find that Troy and Ron had erased my vocals and my guitar so they could add other instruments.

Their only response to my irritation with them was, "Oh, don't worry about it, Turley. You'll sing it again and it will be great."

I was pissed off that I had to re-sing all of my parts, and we lost the incredible magic that we had from the original sessions.

I also realized that signing with Epic/Nashville may have been a mistake. Back then, people around the country believed that everything coming out of Nashville must be Country music. I learned this while doing a promotion in Boston, where the record store I was appearing had "West Virginia Superstar" in the Country Music section. Maybe the title also led to their confusion.

Epic was holding a corporate convention in Nashville and as one of their artists I attended with Troy and Ron. All of the top executives were there, and when one of the bands scheduled to play cancelled, Troy and Ron jumped on the opportunity to get me on stage.

"We've only booked bands to play," the convention organizers told them.

"Don't worry," Ron said. "Once Turley starts playing you'll think you're hearing a band."

On I went, and by the time I was finished I had everyone on their feet, dancing and singing along to gospel and Curtis Mayfield. Afterward, Bruce Lundvall, the President of CBS/Columbia/Epic, came up to me. Lundvall had obviously enjoyed himself and my performance.

"Turley, that was great. You're terrific!" Lundvall turned to Troy and Ron. "The Turley I heard here tonight is the one I want on an album, not what I heard on *Superstar*. Tell you what, we're going to shelve it and make a new record." Lundvall also wanted me to get another producer. I wasn't going to argue.

Ron put in a lot of hard work to find a good producer for me. The first person we talked to was Jim Messina, formerly of the group Poco, who became internationally famous with Loggins and Messina.

It was Jim and Richie Furay who were on the Moody Blues tour with me, listening from the wings when I did my show. Jim had since branched into producing, and when we approached him he invited us out to his ranch in California to work out the details. Jim wanted to produce me, but he wanted me to put together a band to record with. I wanted to work with Jim, so I went back to Louisville to audition musicians. I tried and tried, but this time around there was no Dan Hurley or Randy Ehrlich to hire, and so nothing sounded right. No band, no Jim Messina.

I was also in contact with my old friend Bill Takas, who was now a member of Doc Severinsens's Tonight Show Orchestra. Bill gave Severinsen one of my demos, and Severinsen sent it to Quincy Jones, whose accolades are too numerous to list, but include producing such artists as Michael Jackson and Miles Davis. Jones also arranged and conducted several projects for Frank Sinatra. Jones listened to the demo, said that he loved my voice and yes, he wanted to produce me. The possibility of working with Quincy Jones would have been a dream come true for me but unfortunately he was in high demand and wasn't available for another eighteen months. He was on board if we could wait, and while I was willing, Epic didn't want to wait that long. In the music world, a year and a half is a very long time.

Finally Ron settled the issue by finding a producer named Mike Post, who had won both Grammy and Emmy awards. Mike had produced Kenny Rogers' band The First Edition, and Mason Williams with the Grammy award-winning *Classical Gas*. It turned out to be a good choice, as Mike and I hit it off right away and became great friends. We had a lot of camaraderie when we were together, and we were both athletic and loved sports. Mike was an arm wrestling champ. I was invited into his home and met his wife and kids. We even went jogging together.

I flew back to Nashville and told Ron Bledsoe that Mike and I had got on great and that as far I was concerned he was now my producer. Epic was happy, and I soon flew back to Los Angeles for three weeks to cut my new album in Hollywood's Western Studios.

Epic wanted a James Taylor sound on the album, and their directive to Mike Post was to produce a pop-style "JT" product. The lineup of studio musicians included some familiar faces including Leyland Sklar on bass and Russ Kunkel on drums. Both of them had played in James Taylor's band and on my album *Expressions*. We also had Larry Carleton and Stephen Geyer on guitars and Lowell George on slide guitar. Our backup singers included Herb Pedersen and Joey Scarbury. On two cuts we also had the soon-to-be-superstar, Michael MacDonald. It was an all-star lineup, and with Mike Post at the helm we delivered exactly what Epic wanted.

The album was mixed and ready for release, when a month later I was called to a meeting with Lenny Petze in Epic's New York office. I wasn't sure why the meeting was called, but when Petze greeted me he got right down to business.

"We're not happy with the album, Turley, it's too laid back."

"Too laid back? Isn't that what you wanted?"

"Maybe, but we've decided to make a change. We don't want to release the album the way it is."

I was stunned and all I could think of was how three weeks of hard work was being simply brushed aside as if it were nothing. Hadn't we given them what they wanted?

Petze went on to say, "There's someone I want you to meet." He hit his intercom buzzer and said, "Send in Bobby."

"You know who Bobby Columby is?"

"Yeah, he's the drummer with Blood, Sweat, and Tears."

The door opened and Bobby came in. Petze introduced us, and we shook hands.

Bobby said, "Man, you're a great singer!"

"Thanks, and you're a great drummer," I replied

We all sat back down, and Lenny said, "Turley we want you to record an R&B album, and we want Bobby to produce it."

Perhaps Lenny and Ron realized they hadn't gone in the direction Bruce Lundval wanted when he heard me at the Epic convention, and now they were trying to backtrack. Under normal circumstances this would have been music to my ears, but this time, it just didn't feel right.

"I think we could make a great R&B album together," Columby said.

"Bobby," I said, "I've wanted to make an R&B album since '66, and I bet we could make a good one, but there's one problem." I turned to Lenny Petze, "What about Mike Post?"

"Mike's out," Petze answered.

"Lenny, Mike and I have become great friends. He worked his ass off on this album and now you're just gonna ace him out? Why not give him a shot?"

"We don't think Mike can do it?"

"How do you know? He already gave you what you wanted. Why not give us a few dollars to go back into the studio and let Mike produce me doing two R&B songs and then you can decide."

But Petze wouldn't budge. "We want Bobby," he repeated.

"Bobby, no offense, but I think you can understand where I'm coming from. Mike deserves a shot."

"Turley," Petze finally said, "I think you know the difference between a point-breaker and a deal-breaker, and this is a deal-breaker.

"So if I tell Mike to go to hell, then I can still make the album. Is that what you're saying?"

"Well, I wouldn't put it that way, but in so many words, yes."

"I'm not doing it, Lenny. Mike deserves a shot and I won't ace him out." I stood up and shook hands with both Bobby and Lenny. "Lenny, I'll speak to my attorney, Al Schlessinger, to see what he thinks is best for me."

When I got home I called Mike Post and told him what had happened.

"Oh God, Turley!" Mike said. "You shouldn't have done that. This is business. I would have understood."

"Mike, I couldn't do it. I couldn't let them cut you loose after all the work you did. I consider you a friend and I just couldn't do it. No wonder I hate this god damned business. I just don't understand why this kind of shit happens."

"I'll call them," Mike said. "I'll smooth it all over."

"No, Mike. I'm not making another record with somebody they just shove on me. I've had it. It's done."

Loyalty mattered to me then and it still does today. I'm not sure I could have lived with myself if I had done what they wanted me to do to Mike. I also don't think I would have been able to be fair to Bobby. In the end, I was dropped by Epic Records. Yes, it was a missed opportunity to "make it big," but at least I hadn't turned my back on a friend, and Mike Post has never forgotten it.

Funny enough, a few weeks later I received a check in the mail for a large sum of money from Epic. They didn't owe me the money, and I never found out who decided to send me the check. I can assume, however, that loyalty did matter to whoever made that decision.

CHAPTER 21

Don't get me wrong, I've been blessed with children and family, great times and good friends. I can look back at lot of accomplishments with satisfaction. In between were the disappointments.

How did I keep going? To me, that would be like asking why I keep breathing. In retrospect, I think that my history with my eye surgeries as a child taught me how to deal with disappointment and keep moving forward. That's not to say the eye surgeries didn't work, but as a child, each time I thought I would wake up with clear vision, but that never happened. I think that as an adult, I drew on these experiences and used them in dealing with show business rejections. In my doctors' opinions, each surgery was a great success and paved the way for future surgeries, but the small child didn't understand that. As an adult, I have had several favorite catchphrases, and one is "next to blindness, it's a piece of cake." Each rejection in show business was small when put into perspective. Throw in mom's favorite motto, "defeat is no option," and I guess we have answered the question.

On August 5, 1977, I received a very good reason to keep moving forward when my son, Adam, was born. I made the commitment very early to always be there for my kids. This meant encouraging them, teaching them right from wrong, and telling them that I loved them. All the things that my mom had given to me and my siblings, I would now pass along to my own children.

After the television show, Patty and I had moved to Atlanta to check it out, only to relocate to Nashville when I signed with Epic. Now we decided to take the check from Epic and use it to buy a house in Louisville. With a wife and a baby, I needed to branch out and find more ways to take care of them, and Patty needed the help and support of her family. I had co-produced two television shows, and also produced a 20th Century artist, Mary Welch. I really loved the production end of the business, and I wanted to produce more. I felt that production would give me another avenue to provide for my family, and I had connections at 20th Century due to the success of Mary Welch. I met a couple one night at a party who offered me the opportunity to set up a music production house.

Gil Whittenberg owned the biggest construction firm in the city, and he and his wife, Jo, wanted to use some of their millions to promote the arts, particularly music. The Whittenbergs introduced themselves and asked me if I'd like to produce local music. With their financial backing and my experience and expertise, we would discover and promote unknown talent. We met several times over the next few weeks, and became friends. The Whittenbergs set up an account for me with a generous sum of money and free reign to spend it on regional talent. Our goal was to create demos to be presented to record labels.

The artists I chose were Mickey Clark from Louisville, Sundown Red from Southern Indiana, Tight Shoes from Louisville, and later on SouthShore from South Bend Indiana.

In Sundown Red I thought I had an act that could go all the way. I took advantage of my prior success, and sent their demo out to 20th Century, where its president, Alan Livingston, had an open door for me. The label liked what they heard and offered a contract.

We were in Orlando at BJ Studios recording, when on the third day of recording, the secretary came in to tell me I had a phone call. I left the studio to take the call, and it was Pat at 20th Century. He said he had some really bad news. Alan Livingston had been fired and the new president had cancelled all of their rock acts, including Sundown Red. I talked to Pat for a minute and told him that I wanted to continue to try to shop the band to other labels, and asked Pat to relay to his people that he wasn't able to get me on the phone today. Pat agreed, and I went back into the studio to continue the sessions. The next day, once the sessions were completed, I called a meeting with the band to give them the shocking news.

I tried to get them to not take the rejection personally, and explained to them that seven other groups had been dropped as well. I told them that I wanted to mix the four songs that we had and shop them to other labels and still try to get a deal.

The leader of the band spoke up and said, "Fuck it! I hate the record business and I don't want to do it. I'm done!"

Boy, did that sound familiar! Some guy named Turley did the same thing. I hated to see this young kid make a similar mistake, so I tried to lead him down a better path. He was the only writer, lead singer, and lead guitar player, and without him there was no band.

I turned to the other members and said, "You all need to talk to him, and convince him that you're all part of his decision. I'm going to mix this, and I'll be at the studio tomorrow if anyone wants to come talk to me." I walked out of the room, hoping they would work on him and change his mind.

The next day I went to the studio, and a couple of the players came by and reported that he refused to budge. To this day, I still think he is one of the most talented singer-songwriters that I have ever worked with. To add insult to injury, I had a really good chance for the band to be signed to Warner Brothers because one of their top executives was going to meet me in Miami to listen to them. He loved the tape, and wanted to see them live. Once again, the band's leader refused to play anything but cover music since his announcement that he was through with the business. The executive with Warners told me he wasn't flying all the way to Miami just to see a cover band.

When I returned to Louisville, I had a dinner meeting with Gil and Jo Whittenberg to update them on my progress. I told them the story of what happened between Sundown Red and 20th Century. I also let them know that I had received passes on the other acts, meaning the record labels weren't interested. I truly believe any of these artists could have made it, but the labels just didn't hear what they considered to be a "hit" in any of their songs. I told the Whittenbergs that I believed we either needed to broaden our scope to include talent outside of Louisville, or shut the operation down. I was unprepared for their response, which came almost in unison.

"Why don't you produce you?" said Gil.

"No one in town sings better than you!" said Jo.

I told the Whittenbergs that producing myself would result in more of a financial burden because record labels would expect more than a demo if I was the product. There would still be no guarantee that a contract would be offered.

They didn't seem to be concerned, and asked me for a figure. I smiled and with a little laugh told them it would cost $30,000. This was quite a bit more than the $4,000 budget each of the other acts had cost them. I was again unprepared for—and a bit shocked by—their response.

Gil said, "It'll be in the account tomorrow morning," to which I replied, "you guys are just too much!"

I spent the next two weeks choosing the ten songs to record for the album. I booked some time at Allen & Martin Studios in Louisville with Bobby Ernspiker as engineer. I recorded myself playing two different guitars using a metronome (today called a click track). I also recorded my lead vocal and sang all of the background parts. When that was done, I took the multi-track tapes to Nashville where I overdubbed the whole band at one time, using Gene Eichelberger (*West Virginia Superstar*) as engineer. By doing it this way, I could sit in the control room while the band played, and make sure that they followed my arrangements and stayed true to my style.

The Nashville portion with the band took about ten days, and it was truly a magical experience. I had an all-star cast of studio players including Kenny Malone on drums; Farrel Morris on percussion; Jack Williams on bass; Reggie Young, Steve Gibson, and John Goin on guitars; Shane Keister and David Briggs (of Elvis Presley fame) on piano/keyboards; and Rock Williams on saxophone.

When it was all over, I took them all out for a big after-session dinner where we had a great time making fun of each other as musicians do. Each of the players also made a point of telling me that this session had been the most fun he had ever had as a session musician. Kenny Malone joked that he was having trouble keeping time because the damn metronome was dragging. We all laughed about that. Sometime later I learned that he might have been right because the metronome ran on battery, and they do have a tendency to slow slightly when the batteries are running down (oops).

I spent five more days at Woodland Sounds studio mixing and then headed to Los Angeles where I had appointments with three record labels: Infinity, Portrait, and Electra Records. All three labels offered me the standard contract for the day—one year with four one-year options, an $80,000 budget, a $25,000 signing bonus, and a ten-point production deal.

My friend, Gabriele Arras, a lady I had known since my days with Warner Brothers, often held private parties, and when I was in town, I always called her to see what she was doing. To say the least, I was pretty excited about the offers, so when I called Gabriele, to see what she was up to, I shared my good news with her. I told her about the offers, and she asked me to come by her office and play the album for her.

When Gabriele listened to the tape, she literally went nuts. She came around the desk to give me a big hug, and said, "We need to let Mick hear this!"

At this point I found out how un-hip I truly was when I said "Mick who?" to which she replied "Mick Fleetwood."

"I always thought it was Fleetwood Mac, so it's Fleetwood Mick?"

Gabriele laughed and explained to me that the "Mac" part came from John McVie, who founded the band with Mick Fleetwood.

I asked Gabriele why she thought Mick would want to hear my tape, and she told me that she and Mick, along with John Courage (JC), had formed a management company. She said if Mick and JC loved it as much as she did, then they would offer me a management contract. I told her that it sounded interesting and I would be willing to hear the details. I said I would be in town for three more days, at the Franklin House, and available in the mornings if she wanted to get together again.

Later I had dinner with Mike Post (who also loved the album), and when I returned to the hotel, there was a message that a limousine would pick me up the next morning to take me to Mick's house.

The next morning I took the limousine to Mick's house, which was in Bel Aire. Mick, Gabriele, and JC were all there along with about five or six other people. When I was introduced to Mick, we shook hands. I reached up with my left hand and felt his shoulder, then brought it down to his bicep. Over the years, I learned this was a good way to gauge a person's height and weight. In shock over what I felt, I said to Mick, "Damn! How tall are you?"

Mick replied, "Six-six and a half."

"And what do you weigh?"

"138."

"Damn! If anybody pisses me off, I'm just gonna pick you up and stab 'em"

Mick laughed hard at that, but he seemed to be the only one. Later, when we were inside talking I said, "I felt like some of the other people didn't like that statement about picking you up and stabbing someone."

Mick snorted and said "Fuck them! I'm so sick and tired of 'yes' people and I thought it was hilarious!"

At that point, I felt like the door was open for a potential friendship.

Everyone really loved the tape, and they asked me if I would be interested in having them representing me. We met the next day at the office with their attorney, Mickey Shapiro. I told them to go ahead and draw something up and send it over to my attorney, Al Schlesinger. We all shook hands and I reminded them I would be in town two more days if they needed to contact me. As I was leaving, Gabriele asked me if I would be up for playing a private party at her house the next night. These were always fun gatherings where her guests loved my music, so I readily agreed. We all had a great time at the party and the next morning I flew back to Louisville.

"Mick Fleetwood and me. Mick was my manager for 18 months, beginning in 1979."

A few days later, I got a call from Al Schlesinger and we went over the contract on the phone. He said the contract was basically a standard management contract with just a few items that he would request they change. He highly recommended that I allow him to draw up a letter of intent for their signatures. This was my first experience with a letter of intent, and Al explained that it would give the management company six months to find a record deal, plus outline a dollar amount that I would earn during the first year of our contract. If they failed to secure a record deal in the first six months, then the letter allowed for an extension of no more than another six months. It also established a minimum of $150,000 in earnings for that first year. Once the record deal was secured, only then would we sign the management contract which would run concurrent with the recording contract. I only had one condition; there were a couple of labels that I did not want to sign with.

Within ten days my phone rang; it was Gabriele telling me we had a record deal. These negotiations typically take about twenty to thirty days, so after I mentally picked myself up off the floor, I exclaimed, "Really? With who?"

Gabriele said, "Ahmet Ertegun of Atlantic Records wants to sign you, Turley, but wait before you say no. It's a huge deal!"

I told Gabriele to send a copy of the contract over to Schlesinger, and I would be flying out the next day. As soon as I hung up the phone, I called Al and made an appointment to see him the next day when I arrived.

When I landed at LAX, I went straight to Schlesinger's office. We sat down and Al looked at me and said, "This is really crazy. This is a monstrous contract. Let me read it all to you without interruption." Anyone who knows me, knows this is no small feat he asked of me, but once he started reading, I couldn't interrupt because my jaw was hanging open!

Al began with, "Here are the numbers: a guarantee of six albums, a total funds [budget] of one million three hundred fifty thousand dollars. Fifteen points [a point equals one penny on a retail dollar] up to a million units sold, then seventeen points retroactive to sale one. You, Turley, will be the sole producer on all six albums.

"So! Whaddaya think?"

"I don't know what to think, Al! My first thought is that I don't deserve a contract this big. What do you think?"

Al leaned in to me, enunciating every word: "Turley, I. Smell. A. Rat. I can't find it, but I smell it!"

But, of course, I signed it.

The next day I met with management, and told them how excited I was about the deal, but added, "I feel that I'm missing a true radio song on this album." Mick agreed.

"Mick, can you get some publishing doors open for me right away so that I can find that song?"

He said no problem, so over the next three days I went to seven publishing companies and listened to 407 songs. The 408th song was a song written by Tom Snow and Nan O'Byrne titled *You Might Need Somebody*.

I met with management again the next day at Mick's house and shared the song with them. They all loved it, and we agreed it was the right song. I told Mick I didn't want to go back to Nashville to record. I told him I wanted to use his studio in Santa Monica, with him playing drums for the session. I also asked him if he could find a rhythm section. Gabriele spoke up and offered to call everyone; she set up a start date that was three days out. Among the players were: Tom Snow on piano, Bob Welch (formerly of Fleetwood Mac) on bass guitar and, of course, the incomparable Mick Fleetwood on drums.

After the session, I flew back to Louisville for a couple of weeks to be with my family, then went to Nashville to re-mix three songs. I mailed them out to Gabriele, and a few days later, on a conference call, they all told me that they loved the songs.

"We've got a hit here, Turley," Mick said, "but I have to ask. What does the title of the album mean, *therfu*?"

"Oh, it's the middle of motherfucker."

All I heard through the line was a lot of snorting (Mick's signature laugh).

Then he said, "One other thing, Turley. Lindsey Buckingham would like to do the cover for the album. Oh, and also, I've got approval from Fleetwood Mac, and we would like you to be our opening act for the Tusk tour."

My response was simple, "No shit?!"

All of this happened from the end of April to the end of June 1979, and it was just an overwhelming feeling. It was hard to trust at first but by the end of June, I really thought I was finally going to get the break I needed and, by now, felt that I deserved.

Then the proverbial shit hit the fan.

I guess it was too good to be true. Ahmet Ertegun called my management company and he was incredibly angry. He demanded a conference call with all three managers. After the meeting, Gabriele called me to let me know what had transpired.

"Turley," she said, "I have very bad news. Unbeknownst to me, Mick and Micky promised Ertegun a Stevie Nicks solo album, and that's why our deal was so huge. "Turley, I am so sorry, and I am also extremely pissed off! I've known you for ten years, and I also know you just want the bottom line."

"So what's the big deal? What's the problem?"

"We don't manage Stevie, Turley, and we have no right to offer her to anyone. It was a blatant lie, and no matter how much they might deny it, Ertegun is furious."

"Gabriele," I said, "what is the bottom line?"

"Ertegun is pulling the release of the album, and will not honor the contract."

"Did he give us any kind of out?" I asked.

"Yes, and no," she said. "We can shop to another label, but it has to be the same deal they offered Ertegun, including Stevie Nicks. Or he is willing to tear up the contract and release this one album. Here's our major problem, Turley. Atlantic is obviously pulling the tour support funds for you, so you won't be included on the Tusk tour."

All I could think to say to Gabriele was that I would contact my attorney, Al Schlesinger to see what I should do. I called Al, and told his secretary that it was urgent that I speak with him. Later that day, I got a call back from Al who said, "So! I sense that the rat has emerged."

"Yes" I replied, "and it's a big, fat, hairy one."

I don't know what happened after we hung up, but later that day I got another call from him telling me to fly out to Hollywood so we could all meet.

Three days later, I was back in Hollywood meeting with my attorney who told me a conference call was being set up between management at Mick's house and Ertegun, CEO, and Jerry Greenberg, President, of Atlantic Records, in New York. Al had a court appearance and couldn't meet me there, but he assured me that everything would be okay. He also reminded me to remember all that was said.

When I arrived at Mick's house, they kept trying to convince me that they had thought Stevie would agree to the original deal. I was already angry, and this just fueled the fire. All I could say was, "Regardless, the whole thing sucks! How are we doing the call?"

Shapiro spoke up, "The four of us will be on separate lines throughout the house, and we're going to put you on a fifth line, but it will be muted. We want you to hear what we're going to offer Atlantic."

"So I'm not supposed to speak?"

"We would rather you didn't, Turley."

The conference call began. Ertegun and Greenberg said their hellos on their end, and Shapiro did all of the talking on our end.

"First off," he started, "we are all really sorry this happened, but we really thought Stevie would agree. So here's our proposal: since Turley can no longer open for us on the Tusk tour, Mick wants to take him along on the tour, at his own expense. Mick wants you to hold a press conference in New York, which he will attend with Turley to show how much he supports him. Plus, while on the tour, Mick will stop into all of the major radio stations in each city, with his arm around Turley saying he's the best thing since orange juice."

Ertegun finally spoke, "That sounds pretty amazing, don't you agree, Jerry?" Jerry agreed that it indeed was amazing.

Shapiro stated, "We think that's actually better than Turley being on the tour performing."

Both Ertegun and Greenberg agreed.

Shapiro went on, "So, can we go back to our original agreement for the recording contract?"

"Not so fast," said Ertegun. "I will agree to this album being released. If we can sell 100,000 units, then we will go back to the original contract and pick up the other five albums."

Everyone said their goodbyes and ended the call. We all met in the living room to talk, and I spoke first.

"I agree with Ertegun—it's pretty amazing. So when do I join the tour?"

Gabriele told me that I would meet them in New York City on November 10 with the press conference to follow. She promised she would arrange for someone to be there at all times to assist me. I went back home to Louisville feeling cautiously optimistic about the future. I spent about five or six weeks with my family, enjoying them and making arrangements to be away from home for an extended period. I was still pretty pissed, though, and I also spent a fair amount of time with my punching bag in the basement.

True to Gabriele's word, when I arrived in New York, there was an assistant at the airport waiting for me. He took me to the hotel where Fleetwood Mac had an entire floor rented for ten days.

Once I got settled in, I called Atlantic to let them know I had arrived, and told them to coordinate with Gabriele for the date of the press conference. The next day, I got a call from Gabriele who told me the press conference had been set for three days out. She also told me that Mick and John had met Francis Ford Coppola on the plane from Los Angeles. Coppola had invited the band to dinner that night at a restaurant in Little Italy, and Mick wanted me to join them.

Francis turned out to be an extremely funny man, and a jazz lover who played the drums. We hit it off right away. Toward the end of dinner, I asked Francis if he wanted to hear my favorite Italian joke, and he loved it so much, he stood up and requested quiet in the entire room. "My friend Turley wants to tell an Italian joke," he announced.

I stood and said, "How can you tell you're in an authentic Italian restaurant? If a car backfires, all the waiters dive under the table."

The entire restaurant erupted in laughter. As we said our good-byes and walked out of the room, several people clapped me on the shoulder and told me how much they loved the joke. I was reminded of the wedding I played in 1964 (Doo ya, Doo ya, Doo ya, Doo ya Wanna Dannnnzzz)?

The night before the press conference, I lay in bed fantasizing about everything that could follow this enormous break for me. The next morning, I had breakfast with Gabriele, and we were both in high spirits, excited about what this kind of break could do for my career.

We arrived a few minutes early for the press conference which was set for 11:00 AM. We were there, thirty seven newspapers and magazines were there, but Mick was not there. We sat around and waited awhile, and I tried to keep people talking, but as the time passed, the tension in the room increased.

Finally, I stood up and announced to the crowd, "After all, he's a rock and roll drummer; he's got to be late!"

Everyone laughed, but then Gabriele came back into the room and announced, "I have some bad news. Mick woke up and is very, very sick and is not going to be able to make it."

I heard a lot of disappointed moans in the room. I was all too aware that those thirty-seven newspaper and magazine reporters were there to see Mick Fleetwood, not Turley Richards, but with all the charm I could muster, I stood up with a smile and said, "I'm well known for my gift of gab, so will you still talk to me? Please?"

That broke the tension and there was laughter again. Gabriele suggested that we do some questions and answers, and she would identify each person who wanted to ask a question. I had a ready-made answer regardless of what the first question was, so the first person asked his question.

"I think Mick wears plaid underwear." That got huge laughter from everyone.

After the press conference, the news made its way to Ahmet, and I understand he was livid.

I heard that he said, "The motherfucker has done it again!"

To make matters worse, Mick never made good on his promise, and we didn't walk through the door of one single radio station on the entire tour. As the tour progressed, and I spent more time around the band and the crew, I discovered there was a good reason for this. Mick Fleetwood never went to bed before eight in the morning. Ahmet Ertegun had left the country for a couple of months so he didn't know that Mick had reneged on the radio stations, in addition to not showing up for the press conference. I got a pass for a while and the single was released, but eventually he did find out.

When *You Might Need Somebody* entered the Billboard Top 100 Pop chart (the gold standard for measuring a record's success), it came in at 88 with a bullet. In order to receive a bullet, a record must move multiple slots each week. The second week it moved up to 78 with a bullet, and the third week it went to 68 with a bullet. By the fourth week, the song was at 58 and that bullet was still there. On the fifth week, we moved to 54 with a bullet, but on the sixth week it stayed steady at 54 and the bullet disappeared. On the seventh week, *You Might Need Somebody* came out at 92.

Years later, I would joke that the song now had an anchor attached to it. The next week it dropped off the charts. I had paid $15,000 out of my own pocket to an independent radio promotion man. (An independent radio promotion guy's job is to pitch the song to radio stations.) Now I called him to ask him what the hell just happened. He told me he had never seen anything like this in his entire career of promoting records. At this point I was contacting everyone I could think of to try to make sense of it. My attorney, Mike Post, and Ron Bledsoe (former Vice President of Epic in Nashville) echoed my promotion man's words. None of them had ever seen a record do what mine had done. Week six coincided with Ahmet Ertegun's return to the country and I smelled another rat, and this one was bigger than the first.

The whole thing haunted me for years. Six years later I found out the truth. My dear friend Joe Boyland was a manager whose artists later included Lynrd Skynrd, Bad Company, and Nazareth. Joe had become good friends with Ahmet Ertegun, and over dinner one night, Joe asked Ertegun if he remembered an artist named Turley Richards. Joe told me later that Ahmet said he remembered me, and that I was a great singer and fantastic producer. Joe told me that he asked Ertegun if he remembered what happened with my single that was up on the charts and kicking ass. According to Joe, Ahmet told him that he would always feel bad about it and that he felt that I had gotten fucked between Mick Fleetwood and himself. Ertegun told Joe that when he found out Mick didn't go to the radio stations as promised, coupled with his no-show at the press conference, he became so angry that he pulled all promotion off the record and it died.

Although it didn't change anything, I guess hearing the truth validated what I had known in my gut all along and gave me some closure. Who knows where I might be today if other people's personal vendettas hadn't gotten in the way? I do know that I walked away from the whole experience knowing in my heart that I would never again sign with another manager or record company.

> *Then my dream caved in on me*
> *The darkness robbed my light*
> *But for the first time, I could see*
> *And I did not like the sight*
> *But a man must be himself*
> *No matter what price he must pay*
> *So I let my dream slip from the jar*
> *And watched it fade away.*[4] (Richards 1974)

---

[4] IBID.

CHAPTER 22

Although the experience with Mick Fleetwood and Ahmet Ertegun was pretty awful, it wasn't the end of my world. On September 11, 1980, my princess, Amber, was born. Now I had two children, and had walked away from the record business. I knew I had to keep moving forward to take care of my babies. I was still producing other artists with Whittenberg funds, so now I focused my energy on finding new acts.

I was introduced to SouthShore, a rock band from South Bend Indiana, by Curt Wallen, who was a local booking agent representing them. I was excited to work with this band because it was my first venture into heavy rock. The band had two good writers, and the original songs I heard impressed me. We agreed on a demo contract and I took them into the studio in Nashville.

I wanted to put together a showcase in Los Angeles to get them to play for record labels but the budget didn't allow for plane fare for the band. Curt already had them working a circuit through the southwest, so he put together a schedule that would get them there the long way—playing clubs along the way as they travelled. It would probably take six weeks to get there, so once Curt gave me their schedule, I started working on putting together a showcase for them in Hollywood that would coincide with their arrival. I chose Studio Instrument Rental (SIR) for the studio because they offered three different room sizes for showcasing bands.

The price included full lighting, stage equipment, and a sound engineer. Showcases are usually staggered with two or three during a day to accommodate the time that the different record labels can attend them. One of the benefits I did reap from the connection with Mick Fleetwood was some pretty heavy duty contacts; I was still blown away when I learned that eleven different record labels were attending the showcase.

I was really impressed with the band, and with Curt who handled the band and the PR. They sounded great, and I was really happy with the positive response from the record companies. I heard the band had a good time too, checking out the local music scene.

The following day after breakfast, the band left for the next city so they could work their way back home. I went back to Louisville to wait for a call from one of the labels, and hopefully go into the studio when the band returned.

During the next three weeks, three different labels expressed interest in SouthShore, but Virgin records was particularly interested. I was invited to fly back to California to begin negotiations. We agreed on a standard contract with an $80,000 budget plus a $25,000 signing bonus for the band. I would get $25,000 as well. It was a one-year contract with four one-year options.

With the contract in hand, I was excited to get back to Louisville. As soon as I got home, I started calling the guys with the great news. I had to leave messages for all of them, so I asked each one to call me back ASAP because I had good news.

For three days I waited for a return call, then I made the rounds calling them all again. Still there was no response. I couldn't believe it, and I remember sitting in my house and saying out loud "Here I sit, with a potential five-year contract for these rock and roll assholes, and nobody calls me back!"

But wait! It gets better.

Ten days later I got a call from the keyboard player, and all he had to say to me was, "Whassup?"

Really?

"I left a message for you fifteen days ago, Mike, and I've left messages for all the other guys! What is going on?"

Mike's reply to me, in his kind of slow, drugged voice was "Then you don't know?"

"Don't know what?"

Mike hesitated, "Al and Ron got into a big fistfight on stage and Ron got hurt. The band broke up, and Al and Ron both refuse to ever play together again."

"You're fucking kidding me! Here I sit with a fucking record deal for you guys *and you've broken up*?"

I think that broke through Mike's stupor because he sounded a little clearer when he said, "You got us a record deal?"

"Yeah, but without the two writers, the deal is gone! By the way, if you talk to those assholes, let them know that I also had $25,000 for you all."

Now it was Mike's turn to say, "Oh fuck!"

It was a heart-wrenching experience, but to this day, I am proud of my work. Blindness worked in SouthShore's favor because otherwise I likely would have paid each and every one of them a painful visit. I had lost a lot of money too. Right then and there, I swore I would never produce another band, but of course I did.

I did, however, tell the Whittenbergs that with the bad luck I had experienced, it was a good time to close down the production house. Thanks to the funds from the *therfu* album, the Whittenbergs were satisfied with the outcome and I just didn't want to take any more chances.

We closed down the production house, but through the notoriety I had gained from producing *You Might Need Somebody*, I was offered other projects. One morning I was having breakfast at the Pancake Pantry in Nashville with my favorite recording engineer, Gene Eichelberger. Buddy Huey, President of CBS/Priority Records, a Christian label, came over.

"Turley," he said, "you have quite a reputation for being a great producer. I'd like you to come over to my office to talk about producing my artist, Carman. Can you come over this afternoon around two?"

I agreed to meet him then, but after he walked away I asked Gene if he could give me any input on Buddy, so I would know what kind of person I was dealing with. Gene said he didn't have any personal experience with him, but that he was well-known around Nashville as a corporate executive.

That afternoon I met with Buddy. He sat with his feet up on his desk, and he gave me a detailed background on Carman and said he thought the singer was on his way to superstardom as a Christian artist. He asked me to keep in mind that Christian budgets are not as big as secular budgets, and wanted to know what I would charge to produce Carman.

I paused for a minute, smiling and said, "Three points and your Rolex watch."

I heard Buddy's feet hit the floor as he exclaimed, "How did you know I had a Rolex watch?"

"Buddy," I said, "sometimes God lets me see."

Buddy burst into laughter, and I laughed with him, but then I confessed, "Actually, Gene told me you had one on."

Then I continued, saying, "Buddy, you kind of have an idea what I make producing secular music, so why don't you just make me an offer?"

"The best I can do is $5,000 and three points."

I asked him if the points were retail or wholesale. After all, I was previously on CBS, so I knew they usually paid wholesale, which would cut my earnings in half. I told Buddy that if it was wholesale, then I wanted six points. Buddy told me that he had the power to make the three points retail.

"Great! Then we have a deal. Oh, one other thing. I need all of my expenses covered too."

"Of course," Buddy said.

We shook hands and he told me he would have the papers drawn up and sent to me. I told him to send a copy to my attorney, Al Schlessinger, in Los Angeles. Buddy seemed to be impressed and surprised that Al represented me. I have to say that the mention of Al's name throughout the years demanded respect from the people I was negotiating with, and I was happy to have him in my corner.

Priority Records flew me to Tulsa to spend three days with Carman to listen to his music and make decisions regarding the style of band we would use. Carman told me that he and Priority had an agreement for the album to be a live recording at Lonnie Pierce's church. Pierce was a well-known minister in the Tulsa area.

I negotiated an increase in the budget with Buddy so we could use one of the best recording trucks in the country. The Dream Machine, owned by Full Sail Recorders, was a Winnebago with a full twenty-four-track recording studio that we arranged to come up from Florida. We set a date for the show, and scheduled three days of rehearsal in Nashville.

On the day of the show, we started setting up early in the morning and then went back to the hotel for a short rest. I arrived back at the truck about an hour before the show, and was sitting in the truck listening in as the show started.

When Carman was introduced I heard a sound that was very familiar, but I just couldn't believe I was hearing it in a Christian concert in a church.

I turned to his manager, Steve, and asked, "What's going on here?"

"The girls treat him like Elvis Presley at every concert he does," Steve said.

"That's great for him, Steve, but I wish you all had told me this—we would have hung two more audience mics farther back."

It really was quite a phenomenon that backed up Buddy's claims about his artist going reaching superstardom.

Eventually he was, but it wasn't going to be as a result of this album. The album, *Sunday's on the Way* was doing very well when out of the blue, Priority Records folded and shut their doors. Obviously that was the end of that project.

After that, I produced two artists for Benson Records—James Ward and Ed Raetzloff. All three of the Christian artists I produced made the *Contemporary Christian Magazine* (CCM) top ten charts, based on airplay alone. Unfortunately the labels didn't get the albums out to the stores, so their popularity was not reflected in sales.

I continued to be pursued as a producer and worked with two artists in Atlanta— Whiteface for Mercury Records, and Sheri Henley (no label). Both were outstanding artists, and I was surprised they didn't go further. It never ceases to amaze me that so many great artists can fall through the cracks. It was a pleasure working with these great artists in Atlanta.

Along the way I met Joe Boyland, who would become my closest friend.

While I was working on the projects in Atlanta, I was approached by the owner of a small local concert hall called The Moonshadow. A year earlier, *You Might Need Somebody* had made the top ten on the number one FM radio station in the Atlanta area, and he loved the song. He wanted me to perform at his venue, and while I was performing there ten days later, Joe Boyland, manager of the opening act, came up to talk to me.

Joe told me he "totally freaked out" on my voice. We talked for a while and he asked if we could meet for breakfast. I told him I had to be back in the studio the next afternoon, so he picked me up that morning for breakfast and then dropped me off at the studio later.

During breakfast we made an instant connection. We were both huge sports fans, and huge fans of a certain comedian I hadn't worked with in many years—Richard Pryor.

After I returned to Louisville, and Joe went back to Nashville, we stayed in touch, talking on the phone two or three times a week. That was 1981, and Joe wasn't yet managing the bigger acts that he would eventually handle (Lynyrd Skynyrd, Bad Company, and Nazareth), and he spent a fair amount of his time "courting" me. Joe was constantly in my ear trying to convince me to let him manage me so he could get a record deal.

"Turley," he would say, "I really think I can get a deal for you. Because your hit song is so recent, your name is still known out there."

"Joe," I would reply, "you're the first person since Norman Schwartz that I truly feel like I could trust to manage me, *but* I have so much anger and hostility toward the music industry and managers. I just don't want to go back into that cesspool."

Joe and I remained close friends until he died in 2009. We would call each other often to vent our frustrations about the music business, girlfriends, wives—pretty much anything. One day he might rant and rave, and I would listen; the next day our roles might reverse. Our personalities balanced each other well, and we always made each other laugh. Every conversation was finished with a bit from one of Richard Pryor's routines.

The following year, I got a call from a long-time friend, Jim England, who lived in Knoxville. The World's Fair was in Knoxville that summer, and Jim wanted to tell me about a baseball field nearby that was sitting empty for the summer, and could be leased. Jim thought it would be a great place for us to book outdoor concerts. Jim was an entrepreneur who owned a recording studio, record store, and restaurants in the area and, he was just like me—he was always looking for another opportunity. I told him that I would love to do it, and that I had a friend in Nashville, Joe Boyland, who would be perfect for the venture. I called Joe, who was enthusiastic about the idea, and we coordinated a date to meet in Knoxville.

We met a week later and put together a plan for the concerts. We decided that we wanted to book acts that were "Oldies but Goldies" types. This would allow us to pull our audience from the demographic of people who were attending the World's Fair. It was a great idea, and we would have had a lot of success with it, except we didn't take into account one aspect of the whole thing that we couldn't control: Mother Nature. It must have rained every damned time we had a show. We should have set up Noah's Ark as one of the attractions! On top of that, half the acts didn't bother to show. We ended up having to refund so much ticket money that we decided to close the whole thing down about six weeks into it.

Over the next few months, Joe and I talked a lot about my moving to Nashville. I had sung all of the background vocals on my own albums, and I agreed with Joe that I could pick up some production work in Nashville while also hiring myself out as a background group. It was a good plan, and I needed the money.

I made the arrangements and in 1983, I moved my family from Louisville to Nashville. I had been getting reports from people back in South Charleston that Mom and Dad weren't looking very well, and seemed unhappy since all their children had moved so far away. I called Mom and was honest with her about what the neighbors were telling me. I convinced her to make the move from West Virginia, where they had lived all their lives, to Nashville. Patty told me that within a week of being around Amber and Adam, they had the sparkle back in their eyes. I felt they had something to live for now.

I was still singing around Nashville, but I was starting to have some problems. Somewhere in the middle of the second set, I would become short of breath, and have to finish the set on willpower. I couldn't sing two nights in a row, and studio singing was out of the question. Little by little it became progressively worse.

I had always dealt with allergies associated with living in the Ohio Valley, and initially I thought that the air in Nashville was affecting me more. I went to an allergist and Patty had to learn to give me shots, but it didn't get better.

Joe recommended a throat doctor in Birmingham, and drove me there to see him. He couldn't find anything wrong, and that was when panic set in. I secretly wondered if my many years of singing high energy had taken its toll. I was petrified that soon I wouldn't be able to sing at all. I had always said that if I had been an engineer or an electrician when I went blind, then I would have been finished but singing saved me. Now, seemingly, it too was slipping away.

It was the first time since 1971 that I truly felt blind, and it was the darkest time of my life. I believed that I would no longer be a functioning person, and would be incapable of providing for my wife and kids.

I was doing anything and everything I could to make money. Mickey was working during the week in Nashville, and driving to Louisville for the weekends. For three or four months, I would hitch a ride back and forth with Mickey so that I could work a weekend gig in Louisville. I also worked as many private parties as I could because they typically paid better, and the total singing time was shorter. I had also been doing recording seminars in Winter Park, Florida, for a few years. I would fly down and spend two or three days conducting the seminar at what is now Full Sail University, working with students and teaching music production and recording engineering.

Joe and I decided we would try to find as much production work for me as possible to keep a steady cash flow. He was successful finding work for me, although his methods weren't entirely on the up and up.

Joe arranged for a lunch with a couple of "money guys" who were looking for producers to do three or four projects. The gentlemen were from North Carolina and they were in Nashville for about a week. We were having lunch and I was doing my best to sell myself by telling them everything I had done. I started talking about how I produced my own record, and the success that *You Might Need Somebody* had on the charts. The two guys said that they knew the song, and they knew my name when Joe first contacted them.

I started to say, "Well, depending on the kind of acts you have—" when the song came on in the restaurant.

"Oh my god," I said, "there it is—that's my song!"

I turned to Joe and he said, "Yeah, I found out it's been playing in some of the restaurants as an oldie but Goldie."

Not only did I get that first deal, but they agreed that I would do three or four more projects for them. We shook hands and left the restaurant and Joe and I walked to the car. We were sitting in the car, and I grabbed Joe's arm and said, "How did you pull that off, Joe?"

"What do you mean 'pull it off?' "

"You know, Joe, how did you get them to play the song?"

I could imagine Joe shrugging his shoulder as he said, "I paid them."

Apparently Joe had paid the manager a few bucks and arranged a signal: when he removed his hat, it was time to play the song. Hey, it worked.

During 1983–1984, I saw three more specialists—one at Vanderbilt University, and two others in private practice who were highly recommended. None of them could find anything wrong with me. To say the least, I was completely distraught.

Thank God Mom was in Nashville to step in and do what she did for me when I was young.

"Richard," she said, "you can't give up. You never have, and you never will. You're a great singer, and you will find a way to work around the problem."

After she said this, I looked her right in the eyes.

"You're right, Mom. I have a five-octave range. I'll just change the keys, and stop singing really heavy soul, and I'll make it through an evening."

The next day I met with Joe, and shared with him the conversation I'd had with my mom. He was excited and I could hear the smile in his words when he said, "So! I can look for a record deal now?"

"Joe, in the words of the great Richard Pryor, 'I'm gonna kick your ass.' And the answer's still no."

Joe's response was something that he told me often throughout the years: "Sixty percent of Turley is better than ninety percent of a hundred percent of singers."

Within a week, Joe found five very good paying one-nighters at regional universities. At the same time, I produced four custom recording projects, so I was busy and the income kept my head above water. The voice, though not only wasn't getting better, it was getting a little worse.

The next gig Joe found for me was in 1985, and it was a very well-paying, summer-long deal at a resort outside of Nashua, New Hampshire. Not only was the pay good, but by the second week, I started getting outrageous tips to the tune of more than $400 a night!

In between songs one night, a man with a heavy New York Italian accent (who I later learned weighed more than four hundred pounds), came up to me and said, "Hey! I love dancing to your music! Play as many fast dance songs as you can!"

The acoustics were not very good in the room, and I couldn't place exactly where he was, but I looked where I thought I heard his voice coming from and said, "I will!"

The guy said "Hey! I'm over here. You blind or somethin'?"

"Blinder that a bat," I said.

"Oh man, I'm sorry! That was really rude. I'm sorry. Hey, wait a minute. Is that brandy snifter your tip thing?"

"It is," I said.

"There's no more than five dollars in there!"

"I know" I said, "They don't tip very well here."

"That's just fucking wrong! You play and I'll dance," he said. I felt him reach over and pick up the snifter.

That all happened during the last set and after I finished for the night, he came back up to the stage.

"Hey man! I love your singing man. You're a great singer. Hey look! I got $475 dollars for you here."

"Excuse me?"

"Yeah, I got you $475 in tips! Hey, I gotta go now, but I'll come back tomorrow night," to which I said, "Please do!"

With that, he took my hand into his two hands, and I thought my God, he's huge!

After he left, all the bar workers came up and asked me if I had any idea what he was doing. Although he was enormous, apparently the guy danced like a gazelle. He was dancing and gliding from table to table stopping at each one and saying, "Hey! put some money in for da singa!"

They told me that he stopped at one table where a man was arguing with his girlfriend. When no one noticed him, he tapped the guy on the shoulder. The guy turned around and snapped, "What?" to which our dancer said, "Put some money in for da singa!"

Apparently, the guy arguing with his girlfriend got a little scared looking up at this mountain of a man dancing around, and he threw his whole wallet in. Our dancer opened up the wallet, took some money out for the snifter, and handed the wallet back to the poor guy. That guy came in and did a repeat performance every night the entire summer, and every night I averaged $400 in tips. Rumor had it that he worked for "the boys in New York," but that summer I was glad he was working for me.

The biggest downfall of the job was that I was away from Patty and the kids for almost four months. We decided that Patty would fly up with the kids halfway through the gig and remain there until I wrapped it up. Unfortunately, that trip never happened because the house we were renting in Nashville was sold out from under us. It did offer an opportunity to move back to Louisville, but Patty had to stay in Nashville to pack up the house. The toughest part of the whole deal was telling mom and dad that they had to move again. But they both took it well and said they wanted to go wherever we went.

From New Hampshire, I contacted a Real Estate agent I knew in Louisville who found two rental houses that were a block away from each other. It was pretty much the same set-up we'd had in Nashville, and it was in the same neighborhood where the kids had lived before we left Louisville. I had been dealing with the fear of the loss of my voice and the stress of financial problems for several years. The added strain from the separation during the summer was just too much for the marriage to handle. Two months after we moved back to Louisville, Patty and I were separated. The reasons two people make a decision to end a marriage are always multi-faceted, and no one bears the blame.

Around the same time, toward the end of 1985, Joe entered into a management partnership with a lady in New York, and moved himself and his offices there. He started developing relationships within all facets of the music business, and one of those relationships was with Ahmet Ertegun, CEO of Atlantic Records. After awhile, he had that conversation with Ertegun about Turley Richards, and we already know how that ended. After he told me about his conversation with Ertegun, Joe begged me to let him arrange a meeting.

"Turley," he said, "I just know that if we set a meeting with Ertegun, and sat down with him, he would sign you again. Please let me do this."

"Joe, once again I can't even imagine working with anyone but you, because of the amount of trust I have in you. Now it's different than before, Joe, I have a divorce that's almost final, and I will not leave my kids. I can't leave them. I didn't divorce my kids, and they need me. Besides, I still think the record business is a cesspool."

"Turley, I'm going to respect your wishes, but please know the door is always wide open. From now on, we're just going to be best friends just like we are now. I want you to know, though, that you're robbing the world of a great singer."

"Joe," I said, "I'll call you once a week and sing to you on the phone. Then I'll kick your ass."

CHAPTER 23

Staying in Louisville to be close to my children was the wisest decision I ever made. Sure, my path in the entertainment business was fraught with problems and there were many disappointments along the way, but the bond I had with my kids was the brightest part of my life and made up for all the dark times.

After Patty and I divorced, I moved into an apartment complex that had a large swimming pool where we spent much of the summer. Amber once told me that she and Adam were the most popular kids in the complex because their dad was the "human ride" in the pool. All of the kids would climb on me, often on top of each other, and I would, one by one, bounce them off. One time there were eighteen kids lined up to take their turn being thrown off my shoulders into the deep end of the pool. Thank goodness I knew which way to throw them, otherwise there might have been a lot less laughing and a lot more crying!

We also went to the movies, taking the bus up the street to the closest theatre. My kids got to sit right up front (where all kids want to sit) because it didn't bother my eyes.

Being Adam's father meant teaching him how to shoot a basketball or to swim. For Amber, it meant watching Sesame Street and playing the characters that make up a little girl's dreams and fairy tales. I think I was up to twelve different voices to match the stuffed animals she had lined up around me. Don't think she didn't correct me when I forgot and used the wrong voice for the wrong animal!

In 1988, I married Diane Ray, and after that, we were able to take bigger trips with the kids. My fondest memories include trips to Florida every spring break where I swam with them in the ocean and took them to the water parks where I was the biggest kid there, going down all the slides. We also went to Hilton Head, South Carolina, where the captain of the speed boat turned the wheel over to me, and we sped across the ocean with the kids screaming in delight.

"Turley with Adam and Amber at the beach."

Several times, we drove up to Cincinnati to King's Island, the regional amusement park, where I rode every single ride with them. The best part of these times for me, was that my kids never thought of me as a blind person—I was simply their daddy.

I've never gotten to see my kids' faces with my eyes, but the descriptions that my wife gave to me painted a picture of pure joy as we shared these experiences.

Adam once was asked at what age he fully realized that his father was blind, to which he replied, "My dad's blind?"

Every day wasn't Kings Island and the beach, though. Some days were tough because they were normal kids. One day when Adam was in the eighth grade I got a call from the principal asking me to come to the school right away because Adam was in serious trouble. I called Diane who had to leave work, come pick me up, and drive us to the school. When Diane and I got there, we were ushered into the principal's office with Adam.

The principal said, "Adam, do you want to tell your father what you did?"

Adam grunted and groaned but didn't answer.

I said to him, "What did you do, Adam?"

Adam was still reluctant, but eventually in between what Adam told me, and what the principal said, I got the whole story.

Apparently, Adam was in the cafeteria with four or five other kids who had been given detention for various reasons. They were left unsupervised while the rest of the school attended church. The kids got bored (did I mention they were unsupervised?) and decided to amuse themselves. There was a large mural on the wall depicting an old farm scene, and Adam decided it would be a good idea to draw a penis on the cow. The rest of the kids in detention followed suit, so the end result was a wall mural full of anatomically correct cows. Or maybe that made them steers. I have to admit, I had a hard time keeping a straight face in the principal's office, but the kicks to my shins from Diane helped.

Amber was the more flamboyant of the two kids, and her reactions were a little more colorful. Neither of us remembers what she got into trouble for, but when she was told she would be punished she made a universal hand gesture to me. To this day, I'm not sure how I knew what she was doing, but out of my mouth came, "Don't you give me the finger!"

She was so shocked she ran to her room horrified, wondering if she had been played all along and maybe her daddy wasn't blind! Obviously, she knew that wasn't the case, but she recently told me that she still can't figure out how I knew what she was doing.

Everything changes when you become a parent. If you accept that fact, then the rest can be magic. It's never easy, but it's not supposed to be. All that matters is that your kids know you mean what you say, that they can rely on you and trust you, and that you love them.

Today, Adam is thirty-six, and Amber is thirty-three. Adam has inherited my love of animals and strong work ethic. He has four adopted "children"—two dogs and two cats. He even named the two dogs after my mom and dad. He hasn't found that special lady yet to settle down with and have children, but given all he has to offer, there is no doubt it isn't far off, and he will make me a grandfather again.

Amber has a very successful career as a regional director working with autistic and special needs children. To truly show her intelligence, though, Amber married Brian Badgett, a rock guitar player from West Virginia. Brian has worked at General Electric for seventeen years, and carries on the family business running the Badgett Family Farms with his dad. He has me hooked on his local honey and jam.

Amber is an outstanding singer in her own right. She is also a fantastic mother to Zoey Grace, born May 14, 2010, and Henry Paul, born September 6, 2013. Zoey is my new little princess, and she has completely stolen my heart, but Uncle Adam is her favorite (just ask her). I can't wait to bond with Henry, but it takes a couple of years before the little ones can begin to understand that I can't see them.

It would have been easy all those years ago to take Joe up on his offer and get another recording deal. Had I done that, I would have been gone all the time, travelling all over the country (and possibly the world). Not only would I have missed my kids growing up, I would have been shirking my responsibilities as their dad. Today, there is no father out there who knows that his kids love him with the depth that I do. We have a very special bond and I wouldn't trade that for all the record deals in the world.

I didn't want another record deal not only because I didn't want to be away from my kids, but as I have said, I just didn't want to "swim in the cesspool" again. However, I also was still having trouble with my voice, and no one could figure out what was wrong. Naturally, my thought process took me to the extreme end, and I figured that little by little I was losing my ability to sing. I've often said that I am not a "good" blind person. As an artist, I had always made enough money to pay other people to do things for me, such as driving, housekeeping, and grocery shopping. I never learned braille, and I didn't want to use a guide dog. Even today, I only use a cane if it is absolutely necessary. At that time, though, I truly felt that I was going to lose my ability to earn a living as a performer.

In early 1986, I reluctantly signed up at the Kentucky Department for the Blind Rehabilitation Center. The center taught me how to use the cane, some daily living skills, and basic kitchen abilities. They tried to teach me braille typing (I failed that), and keyboarding (I did quite well at that), and how to use the computer. It was frustrating work, and they got frustrated with me sometimes. I refused to consider their idea that I could work as a sandwich vendor, so they told me I had not yet accepted that I was blind. I felt that I had accepted it—I just didn't want to work selling sandwiches! I have to say, though, that going to rehab changed every aspect of my life, and continues to help me every day. The first time I sent an e-mail I cried. Since the age of twenty-nine, I had been unable to communicate in writing without another person's help. Today, being able to interact with others through social networking allows me to have a connection with the outside world. I almost feel sighted.

While I was in rehab at the department for the blind, I was told that many blind people work successfully as massage therapists. I made a few calls, and was introduced to a holistic group that trained me in massage therapy. I was very successful, and at one time had twenty regular clients. The money was good, but I was a singer, and happily I didn't have to work as a massage therapist for very long.

In mid–1986, I got a call from Mickey Clark telling me that he knew of an ear, nose, and throat (ENT) doctor from Nashville who was giving a talk at a seminar in Louisville. Mickey asked if he could pick me up and take me to hear what he had to say. I am so glad I agreed to go because it changed my life in more than one area.

The doctor giving the talk was Richard Quisling who was well-known for working with country music artists in the area. The walls of his waiting area are covered with pictures of Reba, Garth, and Millsap to name a few.

After the seminar was over, I met briefly with him and explained my problem. Dr. Quisling suggested I make the trip to his office, which I did within a week. Hell, I would have ridden back with him that day if I could have. Mickey drove me to Nashville a week later, and Dr. Quisling found the problem within five minutes. Four other specialists and three years later, this man found the problem in five minutes! I have a genetic condition that, while chronic, is easily fixed in the hands of the right person.

According to Dr. Quisling, there was a tiny tear in my esophagus caused by several years of coughing from various allergies and colds. The problem was compounded by my refusal to give in, and by continuing to sing and push myself, I had developed a small nodule. Surgery was necessary to remove the nodule, and after a short recovery time, my voice returned to normal.

Dr. Quisling saved my career, and I am eternally grateful to him. Whenever I am in Nashville, I have him look at my esophagus. About every four or five years he has to "zap" it again. Although the procedure is uncomfortable, the trips are always enjoyable because Dr. Quisling is such an interesting and nice person. I recently saw him again, and had the pleasure of witnessing his artistic side. He strapped himself into his own invention—a one-man-band instrument that includes a keyboard, drums, harmonica, guitar and synthesizer. We sang *Country Roads* together, which he recorded on his iPhone. (Look for it on the Internet.) According to him, it will come around in about forty years. I'm not sure I really understand his theory, but he does. Once again, I am eternally grateful that I met Dr. Quisling. Mickey, thank you so much.

The other person I was happy to meet at that seminar was Katie Agresta who was a speech pathologist and also a vocal coach. Among a host of other stars, she worked with Cindy Lauper and Jon Bon Jovi. On that day, I had no idea where my future lay, but I took home the material. Little did I know that five years later, I would begin to use them when I became a vocal coach. Her exercises, along with those I learned from Dr. Quisling, became the foundation for the teaching I would use for twenty years—and counting.

CHAPTER 24

In November of 1986, I opened a concert for Ray Charles at the University of Virginia in Charlottesville. Adam was nine years old and made the trip with me. It was a fun road trip with my bass player, Roger Culter, driving us; Adam and I made some great memories. I got to spend time with my son, and I also got to share the stage with one of my idols.

Shortly after I returned to Louisville, I met Diane Ray at a restaurant/club where I was playing. We started dating and eventually Diane and I were married in June of 1988. Four months later Patty and I decided that Adam should come live with me. Not much of a honeymoon, but Diane took it all in stride. Less than a year later, my dad passed away, and my mom came to live with us as well. Diane was twenty-four years old, awfully young to have a pre-teen and an elderly woman under her roof, but she told me that she loved me and my family was her family. I can't begin to express my admiration for her attitude and how good this made me feel.

My dad passed away in September of 1989. He was born Francis Marion Turley. He hated the name, so he legally changed it to Cody Winston Turley long before any of us were born. He chose Cody because he saw Wild Bill Cody in a travelling rodeo and he liked the name. No one is sure why he picked Winston, but he smoked Winston cigarettes, so I guess that's as good a guess as any. In retrospect, he probably paved the way for me, so when I changed my name, there wasn't too much they could say, except for mom who bristled when she was called Mrs. Richards.

He was never sick a day in his life (or if he was, he didn't let on). The day before he died, he got a haircut, washed his car, and called his family on the phone. That evening, he and mom watched their television shows and went to bed, and he just never woke up. Don't we all wish we could be so lucky?

I still remember how mom's voice sounded, though, when she called me and said, "Richard, Cody's dead."

I told her to go straight to another room and we would be right there. When we got there, I found her sitting on her Duncan-Phyfe couch with Amari, the dog I had given to her. Amari's head was on mom's lap. We took mom (and the dog) home, and I made the arrangements for Dad's body to be transported to West Virginia for burial. Mother never spent another night in that house.

Mother lived with us for two years, and I am so happy that God gave me the chance to take care of her. She spent so much of her life caring for me; the scales are still uneven, but at least I got a chance to give some of what I was given back to her.

During that time, she made the trip a few times to the Washington, D.C., area to visit my sister Carolyn along with her husband, Bobby, and their two adult children, Lynn and Robbie. My mom had an amazing sense of humor, and two of her funniest stories came out of those trips.

My sister Carolyn always sprayed pine scented air freshener in her bathroom. One day my mom opened the door to go in and announced in her West Virginia drawl, "It smells like someone crapped a Christmas tree in there!"

The other story happened when we picked her up from the airport. Bobby had given her a box of chocolate-covered cherries, which was her favorite candy. I guess mom didn't know that Bobby had called me and mentioned it in the conversation.

When we collected mom, we asked her where the box of candy was. Mom didn't miss a beat and said, "I fell asleep on the plane, and when I woke up they were gone! I think the woman next to me ate them."

Diane took her out to the car, and while Adam and I waited for the luggage to come around on the luggage carousal, a woman approached us and asked if Mom was okay. When we told her yes, and asked her why she was wondering, she replied with, "She ate a whole box of chocolate-covered cherries and it worried me."

In late September of 1991, Diane and I made a day-trip to Nashville to see Dr. Quisling. When we got back home and raised the garage door, Diane saw a note on the front door. The note was from Adam, and it said that Mom was in the hospital. She had suffered a stroke. She was taken to the hospital by ambulance and Adam had ridden with her.

I called Patty and asked her to pick up Adam, but not to mention anything to Amber until we knew how serious it was. Adam was the one who found her on the kitchen floor, and needless to say he was pretty traumatized. Mom was paralyzed on one side and remained in the intensive care unit for ten days. She was then moved to a nursing home.

I truly believe God kept her with us so that I would have more time to adjust to the fact that she was going to leave me. Many of my friends volunteered to drive me so that I could go see her every day, at least twice and sometimes three times.

One day, I walked into her room and asked, "Mother, how do you feel?"

True to form, in her now garbled West Virginia drawl, she said, "With my fingers!"

She was in the nursing home for ten days, and then she contracted an infection and had to be moved back to the hospital. Mom lived a total of twenty-eight days after her stroke.

Two days before she passed, Bob Russell, minister of my church, Diane and I, and three or four other close friends were visiting and gathered close to her around her bed. Bob asked if he could say a prayer. Bob began his prayer, and after a moment, Mom groaned and tried to talk.

Diane leaned down and said, "Miss Turley, remember now—just one syllable at a time."

Mom struggled to enunciate each word, and said, "Get...back...FART!" The room exploded into laughter, which probably greatly relieved Mom because it covered up the sound of her bodily functions. Two days later, at the end, Diane and I sat on either side of her holding her hands. Little by little, she just drifted off to sleep. I believe I told her to say hello to Kiongazi for me. Afterward they had a hard time getting me to leave the room.

The funeral was in South Charleston, West Virginia, and it was a beautiful turnout for Mom. She had left some written instructions for her funeral in her Bible, and unbeknownst to me, one of them was that I should sing at the service. She wanted me to sing *When They Ring Those Golden Bells*. It was the hardest thing I ever did, and probably the only time that I was glad I couldn't see because I would have seen her lying there.

I stood up to sing, not knowing how I was going to get through it. I remember thinking, "God, you're going to have to sing this for me."

It was truly an out-of-body experience for me. I could hear my voice, and it sounded better than it ever had to me. It was like an angel was singing, which of course is what my mom deserved. When it was over, I literally collapsed into the pew. I was a mess. After the service was over, Uncle Hubert came over to me. Amber was sitting on my lap, crying and I was trying to comfort her. Uncle Hubert had a way with words that belied his West Virginia twang.

"Richard," he said, "your glorious voice reverberated and echoed throughout the halls of this building."

It just struck me as really funny and I was able to laugh for the first time that day.

I lost my dad and my mom within two years of each other, and travelled back to South Charleston for each of their funerals. So many friends and family attended their services, and it was not only a testament to the character of my parents, but also to that of the people I grew up with. It made me proud of my hometown.

My mom was my guardian angel on earth, and she was the one who gave me the perseverance to keep going when others might have given up. "Defeat is no option" was her motto to me, and as her health declined I sometimes wondered how I would go on without her.

As I walked away from her gravesite that day, though, I still felt her in my heart; I realized that she would always be with me. I told the kids the same thing as we walked out of the cemetery.

"Grandma's body might be in that grave," I said, "but her heart, her soul, and her spirit are inside all of us. She is with us all of the time."

As we drove away, we decided not to be sad, but to remember all of the funny things that Grandma did. Those stories carried us back to Louisville, the next day. Not a day goes by that I don't think of her, and talk to her. Her wit and her wisdom continue to carry me through.

CHAPTER 25

Early in 1991, while Mom was still living, I started working as a vocal coach part time. I started with just two or three students I would see at the house. During this time, I was also continuing to work on custom production projects as well as performing regionally at clubs and private parties. Somewhere around that same timeframe, I got an offer to work for a small church as their music director. I worked there for about a year, during which time their membership quadrupled. While I was there I used a programming synthesizer and although it was not designed for the blind, I taught myself how to use it. It was something similar to today's products like Garage Band, and it created sounds like drums, horns, keyboards, and strings.

I found myself at a crossroads faced with a dilemma. I was offered a three-album record deal with a major label out of Nashville. The producers wanted to record me as a country singer. I was considering the offer, because the money was really good and the job with the church had ended. Along came Joe Boyland, who stopped me short saying if anyone was getting a record deal out of me, it would be him—after all, he had been standing in line for a long time!

"Turley," Joe said, "if you're going to sign a record deal, come with me and we'll go back to Ertegun and Atlantic. Besides, you're not a country singer! What are you thinking?"

He was right, of course, and country back then was not what it is today. Had it been twenty years later, I probably would have done it because during that time country started sounding more like pop. Back then, though, it was pure country and I just didn't have that kind of twang. In the end though, Joe's words reminded me of a valuable lesson I had almost forgotten. Every record label out there wanted me to be the next copy of someone who was already big. No one wanted to let me be me, and that was why I had walked away. I needed to keep walking.

Sometime in 1992, I was talking to an old friend of mine, Tom Sobel. Tom had been active in the music scene around Louisville since the late 1970s. He was also well known around town as a pool player and often won local tournaments, so we had plenty to talk about. In 1982 he had booked my band The Numbers and me as a solo singer regionally throughout the 1980s. We had a little incident with a booking at a club with the band in '82, where the owner of the club refused to pay me for an entire week. We had packed the place for the three weeks previous, but I guess he wasn't happy with the crowd for that week. Tom came up with an idea to get me (and him) paid.

I set up my stool and guitar outside of the club with my open guitar case at my feet. I wore Ray Charles style dark glasses, which I do not wear otherwise. We recruited some people to stand around and every once in a while toss some coins into my guitar case. Tom phoned Gary Olmstead, who was "The Troubleshooter" for WHAS (the station my television show had been on). Gary came down to film the action and interview me as I played and sang for "the crowd." We hammed it up for the cameras, and I played up the blind act, even telling

Gary that this was better than selling pencils on the street, and asking passersby if they had seen my dog anywhere.

The station ran the footage on the news that night. I got a phone call the next day telling me the club would pay me, but not unless Olmstead went back on the air to state that I had been paid. We went back and forth a few times over how payment was to be made, but in the end I was handed cash and only then did the station do what the club wanted.

Tom branched off the music scene into comedy acts around 1981. I used to let his comedy acts perform during my breaks when he was getting started. Tom is very hard to tell a joke to because he knows all punch lines already, but for some reason he thought I was funny and told me I should try stand-up. I thought, why not? For about three or four months, I let Tom book me into regional college campuses, and some comedy clubs. I still sat on a stool with my guitar, and would strum chords as I performed. The crowds liked me, and my jokes went over well, but both Tom and I both knew I was a "one trick pony" because all I had were blind stories. Bar none, Tom is the most honest agent I have ever worked with.

Turley with Joe Walsh in 1993. A long-time friend and monster guitar player.

By 1993, I had built my vocal coaching business up to around ten or twelve students who took weekly lessons in my home studio. I was still playing clubs and private parties when I could get them, but I was always looking for new ideas to make money.

I wanted to find a way to raise funds to produce projects and at the same time provide write-offs for the investors. The Venture Capital days were over because of the changes to the tax structure, and there just weren't enough Gil and Jo Whittenbergs to go around.

Sometimes, ideas come from the strangest places. One night while I was watching television with Diane and Adam, a commercial for MCI came on with their newest campaign slogan. It was the "friends and family" concept, and it gave me an idea. What if I could transfer this marketing plan to bands and singers? The idea was to have a party similar to the investment parties I was involved with during the Venture Capital days, but with a new twist. If the artists could gather their friends and family, I would show them how to make a small investment of their collective money into their loved ones' career and it would reduce the overall risk to each individual.

It was a great idea, and it worked! During the next seven or eight years, I produced ten to twelve artists using the friends and family platform. Unfortunately, the majority of the bands refused to record other writers' music, wanting only to do their own original songs. None of them had a song that the record labels thought could be a hit, and it kept them from being signed.

In 1995, after producing a couple of Christian artists, I decided that I wanted to produce my own Christian album. My thought was that I could use this album to kick off a Christian music ministry. Louisville has an incredibly gifted music programmer in Bob Ramsey, and he and I sat down and put this album called *Insight and Out of Mind* together. With the exception of Greg Foresman, Rob Johnson, and me on guitars, every instrument on the album is the creation of Bob Ramsey's programming. In addition, Bob and I sang all of the background vocals.

I gave a concert at Southeast Christian Church to introduce the music, and while the concert itself was well received, the success ended there. The music that I played, while Christian in nature, still was blues and R&B, and the churches felt that it was too "raucous." The black churches loved it.

Two Christian booking agencies, one in Los Angeles and the other in Nashville, wanted to book my Christian music ministry, but if I signed with either one of them, it would have resulted in a lot of time out on the road. Once again, I was at a crossroads, and once again I chose the road that kept me home with my kids.

My vocal coaching business continued to grow, and with Diane's salary, we were able to keep on top of our expenses, but I still wanted to get ahead of the game. Always remembering Silba Turley's motto of defeat is no option, I continued to try to find other ways to make money.

I was introduced to two different companies in multi-level marketing. Going all the way back to my Fuller brush days, I had been successful in sales. Since one of the companies was using CDs as their product; it seemed like a perfect fit and I was doing very well. There were many of us who were doing well—too well apparently. The corporate executives decided to change the compensation package so drastically that our incomes would be dramatically reduced. A few of us were in contact with each other, and we made the trip from our various cities to meet with the executives. We were willing to help out some, if the company was struggling, but we were not willing to accept the changes that were being shoved down our throats. Management heard us out but refused to give or meet us halfway, so we pulled out. The company folded a month later. The other company was nutrition based and, again, everything was going well. For some unknown reason, the powers that be decided to change the formula and the resulting product tasted terrible. Most of the distributors, including me, left the company. Win some/lose some and the moral of that story is stick with music, Turley.

Over the years, all of the ups and downs and the associated uncertainty that is a part of the music business, took a toll on my marriage to Diane. She worked at her own job during the day, and then came home to fix meals, but she still insisted on being there to drive me back and forth to my music gigs. That had to be hard on her, and it also had to be hard trying to stay positive through all of the other ideas I pursued as money-making ventures, but she always helped out. Diane was a great stepmother to my children and she was truly a nice person with whom I got along well. In the end, though, there were problems that were between her and me, and the marriage ended amicably in March of 1998. We remain friends and I wish her the best, and hope she always knows how much I am indebted to her for her total acceptance of my son and my mom when she was a newlywed.

So I was single again for the first time in ten years, which threw me back into the whole dilemma of independent living as someone who couldn't see. Again, the biggest problems were cooking, cleaning, and getting to jobs. This time around, I fared a little better because I had the skills that rehab taught me, and my computer was a blessing. I was able to get bookings via the computer by sending out bios. I got the house in the divorce, so I refinanced it into my name only. W we decided on joint custody of the dogs, so I only saw them every other week.

I was playing a gig at a restaurant in June of 1998, when I was approached on break by a guy from the audience who asked me if I was available to play weddings. My track record for weddings isn't great. I'm currently running five to sixteen for success versus failure, so I almost feel as though I should disclose this when someone asks me to sing for his or her wedding. I didn't tell the guy that, but I did let him know that weddings are quite a bit more expensive than other gigs. I asked him where the wedding was, to which he replied Catalina Island. In California, I asked? I figured maybe the guy was drunk, when he offered me $2,500 plus all expenses paid. So I gave him my card and told him to call me in the morning if he was still interested.

He was, so in August I flew out to California where Jake Butts picked me up and took me to the Long Beach port. There I met the person who had been hired to assist me for the three-day trip. We took the ferry to the island where the bride and groom, Tim and Michele, met me and took me to the yacht where I would stay. We partied that night and I sang for everyone; we had a great time.

The wedding went off without a hitch, and there isn't much to tell about that, until we fast forward to the year 2002. I decided to take Adam and Amber to California for a late summer vacation, and I was scheduled to play one of Jake Butts' private parties. On a whim I e-mailed both Tim and Michele separately to invite them to the party. I received responses from each of them telling me that they couldn't make it, and that they were no longer married. (Add that one to the track record.) I responded to each of them to let them know that the offer stood regardless of their marital status, but Tim was out of town.

Michele, however, wanted to see me the following day and meet my kids. Michele and I ended up dating for several years, and she was a lot of fun to be around. She often forgot that I was blind, which is the highest of compliments to me; but it can result in some funny situations. We were shopping one day in Walmart, with me pushing the cart and Michele guiding it from the front end, when she spotted a blouse or something that she wanted to look at. Unbeknownst to me, she walked away from the cart, which I naturally kept pushing.

The next thing I knew, I ran into something and a voice said, "Can I help you?"

"What is this?" I asked.

Michele, realizing her error, ran over to the cart saying "Oh my God, Turley, I am so sorry!"

"Where are we? I asked. "What did I run into?"

Believe it or not, I had run directly into the optometry counter!

When she told me where we were, I didn't miss a beat. Turning toward the voice behind the counter I said, "I need glasses!"

Michele also liked to go to the beach where, much to her dismay, I insisted on going body surfing. Without being able to see, I had to feel the undertow, which told me when the next wave was going to hit. On that particular day, I had successfully ridden fourteen waves and only been knocked down twice. I was feeling particularly cocky and was standing sideways bragging to Michele about my wave riding prowess.

I yelled out to Michele, "Fourteen to Two! The bitch of the sea ain't got a chance..."

I was immediately knocked down by what onlookers told me was an enormous wave that took me head over heels. I landed on my ass and slid ten feet up onto the beach. It must have been a pretty spectacular fall, because Michele and the onlookers came running over yelling.

"Oh my God, Turley, are you okay?"

I was sitting with my elbows on my knees, and I snapped the fingers of one hand saying, "All right!" I jumped up and ran back into the ocean. I think I carried some kid's sand castle back into the water in my shorts.

In September of 2002, Jake Butts called me to say that Rusty Hale had set me up to perform for a Bob Dylan tribute at the Bohemian Club in San Francisco. The Bohemian Club was founded in 1872, and is a private men's club where high powered businessmen and artists meet to relax and forget about their day-to-day life. Apparently Bob Weir of The Grateful Dead had to cancel, and Rusty had recommended me for the gig. They loved my music and my singing and throughout the next three years, I performed at their annual gathering at The Grove held during the summer in Santa Rosa. It was there where I had the honor to perform *Eleanor Rigby*, backed by the San Francisco Philharmonic String Quartet. The performance was so well received that I was asked to repeat it at the club in San Francisco during one of my two additional shows there.

Between my old friend Jake and my new friend Michele, I began to get bookings for corporate events in California. Most people who are hired for corporate parties have some form of merchandise for sale there—usually a CD or a book or both. I didn't have anything current, so I realized that it would make sense to put something together. I had been writing music all along thinking of an R&B/soul/blues project. Over the years I have written about 650 songs, but with the exception of three songs, all of the music on *Back to My Roots* was written for that CD.

I produced, wrote, and arranged all of the songs. I recorded *Back to My Roots* in Louisville, and mixed it in Nashville with Gene Eichelberger. I had told Joe Boyland that I would send the final mixes to him once they were complete, which I did toward the end of 2006.

I recall saying to him, "Joe, I've got these finished and I'm going to send them to you. If you still want to get me a deal, I give you permission to do so."

Joe's response was classic, mixing his own humor with that of our favorite, Richard Pryor. "Well, I'll be a motherfucker! He wants me to get him a deal now. Turley, you're sixty-five years old an' you wants me to get you a deal!"

He loved the CD, but we both knew that at this point in my career, it would be pointless to approach the big labels. We agreed to send it to some of the smaller blues labels where, because of Joe's reputation in the business, the heads of the labels listened to the mixes.

A few weeks later, I got a call from Joe telling me that three labels wanted the CD. They were Alligator, Dixie Frog, and Blind Pig (I thought that one would be a really good fit). They all wanted the CD, but the problem was that as small blues labels they had no artist development money. These types of labels rely on the artist playing at least one hundred dates a year, and I hadn't been on tour since 1980. I also had no band put together to go on the road with, so we couldn't secure a deal with any of the three labels. Joe had predicted this might happen, but it had been worth a shot. To add insult to injury, the economy tanked at about the same time, and one of the first things to go was the big corporate parties. I had a lot of CDs in my garage. Okay, Mom—defeat is no option. So, back to the drawing board.

CHAPTER 26

I think the biggest lesson I have learned over my lifetime is that life tends to balance itself out between happy and sad events. As I reflect on each decade, this seems to be the case, and the 2000 decade was to be no different.

In 2004, I met David Nuckols, a man who through his work would bring me more into contact with the sighted world. David is a computer genius who is the Senior Consultant for Flexera Software, but also is the owner and CEO of Glorykidd.com where he has many clients, including me. He created my website, became my webmaster and, to me, David is a godsend. Going to rehab taught me the basics of computers, but David taught me how to blog, send e-mails, and how to navigate the Internet. He picks up the phone, always greeting me with, "Turleyman!" and is ever willing to help. Even more important to me is that David has become a great friend.

One of the benefits of being more connected on the Internet was the ability to attract new vocal students. Regardless of the economic downturn in 2008, my vocal coaching business continues to thrive, and I keep a steady average of twenty students ranging from age nine to sixty.

A few years ago, I started inviting my students to come sing with me at the clubs where I still play around town. I usually have two students who sing three songs each during the two sets. This gives the students a chance to get the experience of performing live (and trust me, singing karaoke is nothing close to singing live). Plus they get to have a former recording artist as their back-up guitarist! Seriously though, the students get to perform, but still have the safety of my being right there with them; and there is a bit of prestige that goes along with performing with me onstage. I'm very proud to say that throughout the past few years, two of my former students have been contestants on *American Idol* and *The Voice*. The first one passed the preliminaries and "made it to Hollywood" three consecutive seasons on American Idol, and the second made it to the final 20 on *The Voice*.

As I said, life balances itself out. In 2009, on March 18th, the 63rd anniversary of the accident that cost me my left eye, my dearest friend, Joe Boyland, passed away. That night around 10:00 PM Nashville time, we were on the phone, talking about all the things we loved to talk about—sports, jokes, women and, of course, Richard Pryor. When we hung up the phone, Joe was in great spirits, and the last thing I heard was his laughter. The next morning, I received a phone call telling me that Joe had suffered a heart attack. The estimated time of his death was before midnight. I'm sure I was the last person to talk to him. This one truly knocked me for a loop. To this day, I reach for the phone to call Joe and tell him a joke. I really miss you, Joe.

As if losing one best friend weren't enough, three weeks later, I had to put my last Rhodesian Ridgeback, Kiambi to sleep. He was thirteen years old. With Joe and Kiambi gone, I felt more alone than I'd ever felt. It was truly one of the lowest points of my life. I prayed to God for relief from the all-consuming sadness and lack of direction my life had taken.

In late summer the scales balanced again when my daughter Amber told me she was pregnant. Zoey Grace Badgett was born May 14, 2010, and became my Princess II—Amber will always be my Princess I. The balancing force in my life moved from the oldest to the youngest. It used to be my mom who would pull me out of the darkness, but this time it was my granddaughter. I can't begin to tell you how much light that little girl has brought into my life.

The birth of my granddaughter brought me out of my funk, so when I was contacted about doing a radio interview, I was open to the idea. One of my former drivers, Rick Alexander, who remained a friend contacted me from Orlando in late spring of 2010. He set me up with a woman named Linda Derr who had a podcast radio show and wanted to interview me. After the interview, she asked me if I would mind holding for a moment on the phone, so she could take care of another matter, and then talk to me more.

When she returned to the phone she said, "My God, Turley, your life is a million stories. You should write your memoirs."

I told her I wouldn't know how to begin, so she gave me the name of a publishing agent in New York, Jacqueline Grace.

I called Jacqueline a week later, and she agreed that I had a good story, and wanted to represent me. She gave me an outline, a kind of "how to" to begin writing the book. She proceeded to try to find a ghost writer, and told me that in the meantime I should get a digital recorder. She gave me an outline to follow and told me to narrate my life and stories into the recorder. The next step would be to find someone to transcribe those recordings onto paper. This would be the material that I would give to the "ghost writer," who would use them, along with one-hour weekly telephone conversations with me, to put my words on paper. She cautioned me to always remember to keep "my voice" throughout the book, and to remember that I had the ultimate say in how it was written.

The first part of her formula went pretty quickly. I do love to talk, so the recorded portion was completed without too much delay, and I found a great transcriber in my friend Michele in California. The delays began when we started interviewing ghost writers. The range of expertise among ghost writers is vast, and the pay scale goes along with it.

After interviewing and passing on several possible writers, through unrelated conversations, I found the son of an old friend. He was interested in the project and, although he had no experience with writing, he asked me to give him a shot. We agreed to move forward, I sent him the transcripts, and asked him to send a sample back to me so I could forward it to Jacqueline. Neither one of us knew what we were doing, but Jacqueline liked the nuts and bolts of what she read, but cautioned me that it just didn't sound like . . . well, "me"! Once again, the word "unfortunately" comes into my story, but the fact of the matter is that, unfortunately we were taking so long to produce the product that the one-year contract I had signed with Jacqueline ran out, and she decided not to pick up the option.

Obviously it all worked out in the end, because you the reader have the finished product in your hands. The scenario changed once I had someone who began editing the book for me, bringing my voice back into the forefront. Her work caused me to realize that a change was necessary in order for me to be happy with the finished book. Or maybe I should say to even finish the book. After all, we are looking at three years now, and I am seventy-two years old.

The pendulum swung the other way again when one day when I was talking on the phone with my old friend Jim England. I was telling Jim about the book, and that in order to generate interest, I needed to arrange some sort of speaking tour. Jim told me that he knew someone who booked speakers and said he would make a phone call and try to get us hooked up.

I talked to David Wright a few times on the phone, and travelled to Gatlinburg to meet him and, at his request, attend a portion of one of his workshops as a visitor. During that visit, we shot a twenty-minute video of me talking about my life experiences and, of course, singing a few songs. The video will be used for promotional purposes.

David and I hit it off right away with a shared love of jazz. David told me that my celebrity, coupled with my life story, will make me very successful as a keynote speaker, to which I said "book me."

At this writing, it is his intent and my hope that he will publish this book and find lot of work for me as a keynote speaker. Everything seems to be moving in that direction, and it sure would be nice to keep that pendulum on the plus side for a while. If the book has any success at all, it could open a lot of doors for me and help me get back to what I do best—performing in concert. I got a little taste of that in July of 2011, and I want more.

CHAPTER 27

They say "you can't go back home again," but in 2011 I did just that, and created some wonderful memories for my children and me in my hometown of South Charleston, West Virginia.

Jim Snyder is a promoter in West Virginia, whom I met during a short time period when he lived in Louisville. He called me one day in early 2011 to ask me if I would consider coming back to do shows in the region. I was willing, but Jim wasn't able to put enough shows together to keep me in the area for two for three days in a row. He had put the idea into my head, so I called Bob Anderson, Director of the LaBelle South Charleston Convention Center. I used to live down the street from him. I told Bob what I wanted to do, and he was really excited about the idea.

He said, "Richard, the city of South Charleston, and our convention center will give you the LaBelle Theatre for free." I thanked Bob for his kindness, and then called Jim Snyder to tell him the news and that I would like for him to handle the promotion.

Jim handled all of the promotion for the show, which meant going the extra mile since he lived two hours away from South Charleston. He created fliers and posters, and found the stores that would allow ticket sales. He arranged for me to promote the concert by singing at the local coffee shop, The Daily Cup the night before. He also set me up for an interview with the evening newspaper, *The Daily Mail*. Jim's efforts paid off and we were rewarded with a sellout crowd for the concert Saturday night.

Jim really went the extra mile for me. He placed a phone call to Mike Lipton, the President of the newly formed West Virginia Music Hall of Fame. He told Mike that I was coming in for a concert, and that he really believed I should be nominated for the Hall of Fame. Mike agreed, got my contact information, and called me to talk. During the conversation, we set up a time to sit down after my sound check at the LaBelle on the day before the concert so Mike could interview me. I will always remember the day Adam and I arrived at the LaBelle:

"We're here Dad," Adam said as he parked in front of the theater. He read me the marquee: "*Warner brothers and Atlantic Records: Turley Richards concert April 2, 7:00 PM tickets here or at the Daily Cup.*"

I got out of the car and Adam was right there for me. Adam knows the drill, but this time I could turn the tables a bit.

"Do they still have that high curb right here?" I asked Adam.

"Yep," he answered.

"And the ticket booth and the double doors are right in front of us?"

"Sure are," Adam said.

I could picture the old lobby and the ticket booth with the concession off to the side. We walked through another set of doors and we were in the theater. It brought back a thousand memories of when I was a young boy, but the stage seemed closer now as we walked down the aisle.

Bob Anderson greeted us and gave me a hug saying, "Welcome back to South Charleston, Richard."

I had to smile because I hadn't been called Richard very much since Mom died. In West Virginia it comes out as "Rayitchard."

As Adam found the stage door and propped it open he said, "Wait here, Dad. I'm going to pull around back and start unloading." Jim Snyder, the camera crew who filmed the show, and Mike Lipton surrounded me to say hello, and ask how the drive was from Louisville. I told them Adam should be rested and ready to unload since he slept most of the way, and everyone laughed.

"Dad," Adam called from the stage, "I think we're ready. You should come up. The steps are on the right"

Adam met me at the top of the steps, and we went to center stage. Within a few minutes he had everything set up, and all I needed to do was plug in my guitar for the sound check. Adam has my height and strength, and I can leave all of the heavy work to him. I told Adam to let Mike know that I would be finished with the sound check in thirty minutes and we could start the interview then. There's no one I can rely on or trust more than my two children, and both will be here with me for my homecoming to West Virginia. My daughter Amber, her husband, Brian, and my Granddaughter, Zoey, would arrive that evening. During the concert, Amber was going to join me on stage. I was back home and with my family.

While Adam relayed the message to Mike, my mind wandered, and I remembered different times I had been in the LaBelle growing up. I was seven or eight when I got up on the stage to entertain the crowd. Every Saturday and Sunday from grade school through high school, was spent at the LaBelle. I suddenly felt nostalgic, maybe because it was one of the few places around town where I didn't get kicked out.

I sent Adam out into the theatre to check out the sound from different vantage points. Everything sounded great. Jim Snyder, who was not only a promoter but also an outstanding singer and guitar player, was opening the show for me, so I turned the sound check over to him. Adam and I walked out to the lobby to find Mike so we could begin the interview.

In the lobby the camera crew was waiting with Mike. Settled into a chair, he made me feel comfortable with some more small talk until the cameramen were ready. I could feel everyone around me, quietly relaxing while waiting for Mike's interview to begin.

Thoughtful and intelligent, Michael Lipton is a songwriter/musician. His questions took me back to my years in the city—my music, songwriting, and producing, and opinions of contemporaries—then back again to my roots in the Kanawha Valley. Mike was a fantastic interviewer and a professional who asked great questions about my career. We were both very pleased with the interview.

Later that evening, Adam and I drove over to the Daily Cup on the corner of 7th and D Street. I could remember everything around this little corner and exactly how it looked. Before it was the Cup, the street level floor was an old Savings and Loan. The vault was still there behind the counter, but now it was for securing dishes and silverware. Directly across 7th Avenue was the Indian Mound, just as it's been for centuries. But Adam told me that "nearly everything else that I remember is now gone; the basketball court, the concrete stage, the Mound Movie Theater, Thebetts Bar for South Charleston's hard drinkers," and most of the stores and shops my mom always relied on. Gorbey's Music was still there, just a few doors down on 7th, and I'll take it on faith that the Kanawha River was still just on the other side of McCorkle Avenue.

The crowd started to come in, and besides the regulars I found myself meeting and talking with friends I hadn't seen in many years. They all came to hear Richard Turley sing again. Among them was Don Hill who had formed "the Montereys," from Stonewall Jackson High School in Charleston. The Montereys were the rival doo wop group to my Five Pearls. Also there was Rabbitt Jones, who as a young man I saw play at The Crazy Horse Club. The Crazy Horse's customers were mostly black and they went there to hear Jazz, which was the style of music I couldn't get enough of. Before long, Rabbitt was playing in one of my bands. Seeing my old friends added to my anticipation of the concert, and I was really looking forward to seeing more of them, like Jim Bruer the next night.

Finally, Eskew and Turley cousins—some of whom I had never met—introduced themselves, and the Daily Cup was full. It was time to sing so I made my way to my stool and, picking up my guitar, I talked and joked a little bit with the crowd. When I started singing, it was effortless—just like Malachy's, the Back Fence, the *Tonight Show*, or even the Royal Albert Hall.

> *It's so nice to come back home again*
> *It's so nice to be here with all my friends*
> *It's so nice to turn back the pages in my mind*
> *It's so nice to come back home**

As I said, we had a sellout crowd for my homecoming concert. The overwhelming feeling of love and friendship from that night stay with me today.

So many old and new friends and family were at the concert. Old friends like Jim Bruer, Bill Holdren, and Rabbitt Jones, whom I made music with when I was growing up. New friends, like my webmaster, David Nuckols, who had made the trip from Huntsville, Alabama. My daughter, Amber joined me on stage to sing (and damn that girl can sing!) and Adam worked the merchandise at the back of the room. There were tears and laughter throughout the evening, and we all left the LaBelle feeling a little richer for the experience.

For those of you who have stuck with me, and are still reading this book, you can see that I have had a long career full of ups and downs. Today, I feel totally blessed. I have a wonderful family, a very special lady, and I've met people who are lifelong friends. I have made some good music along the way. I call that success.

When I first spoke to the publishing agent in New York who told me that my book would be inspirational to others, I didn't understand what she meant. I always thought I'd just done what I had to do, but the journey of writing this book during the last three years has allowed me to have a clearer picture of what she saw. I had to revisit a lot of old memories in order to write it, and sometimes reliving the memories, many of which had been buried for years, was really painful. But if my experiences in this book help just one person, then it will have been totally worth it.

As I look at you through this book, the most important message I want to leave you with is:

Here I am it's been years since '64
Once again, I have that burning desire
I'll make good music and sail it down a magic stream
And from my wishing well, I'll draw upon my dream,
West Virginia Superstar.

And

DEFEAT IS NO OPTION!

"Promo picture for the 'I'm Coming Home" concert in 2011
at the La Belle Theatre in South Charleston, West Virginia"

"Turley with his soon-to-be wife, Laura and Scott and Jaime Estes in Florida.
Scott was his driver in the 1980's"

"Turley with his son, Adam, his daughter, Amber, and his granddaughter, Zoey at Easter 2013.
Brian took the picture, and we didn't meet Henry for five more months."

ABOUT THE AUTHOR

In 1969, Turley Richards appeared on The Tonight Show with Johnny Carson. At the end of Turley's performance, when Carson stopped clapping, he turned back to the audience and the cameras and said "I think you may hear a lot from that young man, Turley Richards."

Over the years, Carson's prediction came to life. Turley's musical abilities have been lauded by people like Mike Post who wrote the television theme songs to Magnum P.I., The Rockford Files, Law & Order, and NYPD Blue. Mike said, "Turley is a drop-dead, great singer...what a talent." Longtime friend Joe Boyland, who managed the rock group Lynrd Skynrd and was instrumental in the first hits of Mariah Carey and Celine Dion said "I...appreciate and respect his integrity and professional attitude. Turley always wants to make everything as good as possible...this makes for good music. I highly recommend him." On a personal note, Turley considers one of his highest compliments throughout his long career to be when, as a mature man, an entire room of high-powered men were humbled to tears during his performance in Santa Rosa, California.

Today, an active Turley Richards is still performing at small concert halls and night clubs as well as corporate functions, where he combines shows with lectures. He grants interviews on television and radio shows, and conducts songwriting seminars. His vocal coaching business is in its 20th year, and he also teaches songwriting skills to new writers as well as providing consulting and career guidance to bands and singers. Several of his vocal students have made it to the final performances on the television shows, "The Voice" and "American Idol."

Turley is still writing songs that tell his story and are added to his impressive collection of over 650 original works. Turley Richards lives in Louisville, Kentucky with his wife, Laura where he is still close to his two children and grandchildren.

In the end, it appears that the great Johnny Carson spoke the truth. The world continues to see a lot of Turley Richards.